DEGAS

in Search of His Technique

DEGAS

in Search of His Technique

DENIS ROUART

SKIRA

RIZZOLI
NEW YORK

Published in the United States of America in 1988 by

Rizzoli INTERNATIONAL PUBLICATIONS, INC.
597 Fifth Avenue/New York 10017

© 1988 by Editions d'Art Albert Skira S.A., Geneva

Translated from the French by Pia C. DeSantis,
Sarah L. Fisher and Shelley Fletcher

Library of Congress Catalog Card Number: 87-36083

ISBN: 0-8478-0949-8

Printed in Switzerland

CONTENTS

PUBLISHER'S NOTE

There is probably no surer way to surprise an artist's secrets than to study his technique, to follow up his experiments with his medium, to trace one by one the obstacles that his hand had to overcome before reaching the truth dictated by emotion. To analyze the procedures used by an artist in the course of his career is not simply a matter of unearthing forgotten recipes. It is, on the contrary, an attempt to understand that fundamental operation, verging on magic if you will, which enables the creative artist to transmute the resistance of his medium into that moment of pure spirituality which arises from the contemplation of a work of art.

Denis Rouart's book *Degas in Search of His Technique* answers the questions that the committed lover of painting is apt to ask himself before the picture, recognizing in the struggle of the artist's sensibility with the specific instruments of his language the true focus of art and its underlying mystery. Denis Rouart's approach, at once impassioned and scientifically based, thus helps to show that, by resorting to new technical procedures and combining pastels, oils, drawing and monotype in ever varied ways, Degas reveals in fact an unappeased and creative restlessness of mind, spurring him on to decisive challenges and ever renewed hopes of fresh progress. His tireless, his inventive curiosity drove him to experiment endlessly with the mediums and instruments at his disposal, to seek out and test again and again the exact *speed* adjusted to his inner requirements and capable of recording the flashes and tremors of perception that impinged on his eye.

No one was better qualified than Denis Rouart (1908-1984) to make this inquiry and gather precise information about the habits and preoccupations of a painter who jealously guarded his privacy. For he was the grandson of Henri Rouart, a collector and painter who had been an intimate friend of Degas's from their school days and served in the same regiment with him during the Franco-Prussian War of 1870-1871. On his mother's side Denis Rouart was the grandson of Berthe Morisot and the grand-nephew of Manet. So that he had close family connections with the Impressionists and from boyhood moved in Impressionist circles. Later, as a museum curator and art historian, he published monographs on Berthe Morisot, Renoir and Monet, the correspondence of Berthe Morisot with her family and friends, and contributed to the monumental catalogue raisonné of Manet's paintings published in 1975.

This study of Degas's technical experiments, first published in Paris in 1945, has established itself as a work of reference. It was time to publish a new edition, both in French and, now for the first time, in English. This has been made possible thanks to the generous comprehension of Madame Denis Rouart, to whom the publishers would like to express their grateful thanks.

Self-Portrait, c. 1862. Oil on canvas.

INTRODUCTION

In order to understand certain nineteenth-century artists' preoccupation with technique, one must remember that at that time the painter's craft was passing through a critical period. The tradition of apprenticeship had already been much compromised during the course of the eighteenth century and ended by disappearing completely at the century's close. David only aggravated this condition by his desire to make a *tabula rasa* of all that had been produced previously. He did not limit his reformist's ardor to choice and composition of subject, nor to a style of drawing and painting, but expanded it to encompass technique. Claiming to scorn his masters' teaching in this area, even though he had used it so successfully himself, he did not believe it his duty to transmit this baggage to his students. He is in part responsible for the academicism which during the nineteenth century came to replace the teaching of craft in the studio-workshops.

It is possible that this absence of a tried and true technique did not hurt the artists but permitted them to assert their originality to a certain extent. Even though it may seem that such originality could manifest itself in style, conception and interpretation rather than in technique itself, it is obvious that their ignorance of craft brought great torment to the modern painters.

One finds examples of this among the greatest of the moderns.

The *Journal* of Delacroix shows how deeply he was preoccupied by this question, recounting his ceaseless researches in the area of technique and the experiments that he tried in all genres. These experiments were not always conducive to the successful preservation of his canvases, but prove how much Delacroix felt the lack of a sure and infallible craft such as that enjoyed by Rubens or the Venetians whose rich and powerful coloration Delacroix periodically attempted to rediscover. Although he spent a lifetime in violent opposition to the use of conventional procedures and formulas in art, he nonetheless deplored his generation's lack of craft techniques, as shown by this entry in his *Journal*: "I then went to the museum. Two or three days before I did a session there. I highly prize the room of the modern French school. It appears very superior to the one which immediately precedes it. All those who followed Lebrun and above all the entire eighteenth century is nothing but banality and repetition. In our moderns, depth of meaning and sincerity burst forth, even in their very mistakes. Unfortunately, their craft does not reach the height of that of their predecessors. All of these paintings will soon perish" (Sunday, 13 September 1857).

Manet, whose execution appears so facile and self-assured, is a good example of a tormented modern since he himself said that unlike Titian and Veronese, he did not possess a craft that would allow him to indefinitely rework a canvas so that he could bring it to perfection. In a letter to her sister Madame Pontillon, Berthe Morisot relates that while Manet was painting the portrait of Eva Gonzalès he scrubbed away the head twenty-five times in succession in order to be able to work on a blank canvas at each sitting: "In the meantime, he begins her portrait for the twenty-fifth time, she has been posing every day, and in the evening her head is washed away with black. There's what's encouraging for asking people to pose!" In another letter she wrote: "For the quarter hour he concentrates all his admiration on Miss Gonzalès, but her portrait still doesn't advance, he tells me he's at the fortieth sitting and the head is again erased, he is the first to laugh about it" (Berthe Morisot, *Correspondence*, 1950).

Manet: Portrait of Eva Gonzalès, 1870. Oil on canvas.

Antonin Proust writes: "During the course of this year 1879, Manet has been haunted by two fixed ideas, doing a work about the out-of-doors but about the entire out-of-doors, where people's features dissolve, according to their expression, into the shimmering atmosphere, something even more vibrant than *Skating* or the *Boat in Argenteuil,* and dashing off my portrait on a white unprimed canvas in one sitting. So at the same time he embarked on *Father Lathuille,* perhaps the most astonishing work that he has done, and my portrait. After having used seven or eight canvases, the portrait came at one sweep" (*Souvenirs*, 1913).

The expert execution of this painting makes it clear that for Manet, the desire described by Proust did not only correspond to the taste for the unfinished sketch then in fashion, but also to a real need. Moreover, the method Manet employed is a *tour de force* which would not have worked for a large composition.

In the conversations that he had with his friends and disciples Renoir constantly returned to this important question of technique. Indeed, different styles which he practiced during the course of his career owe a great deal to the research of a craft which he lacked and of which he felt an imperious need. Albert André wrote: "He angrily regretted the past

Manet: On the Beach, 1873. Oil on canvas.

epochs when, after a real apprenticeship, one entered into the life of a painter solidly educated." André continues, quoting from Renoir himself: "In reality we no longer know anything, we are sure of nothing. Until one looks at the works of the masters one can't even try to appear smart. What admirable workers those men were, how much beyond us all! They knew their craft! Craft is everything. Painting is not made of dreams. It is first of all manual labor and it must be done like a good workman. But it has been completely overturned. Painters believe themselves to be truly extraordinary beings, they imagine that by putting blue in the place of black they will change the face of the world.

"For my part I have never permitted myself to be revolutionary, I have always believed and believe still that I can only continue that which others have done much better before me" (Albert André, *Renoir*, 1928).

To Vollard, Renoir said: "Today we all have genius, that's taken for granted. But what is certain is that we no longer know how to draw a hand, and that we are completely ignorant of our craft. It is because they were sure of their craft that the masters could have this wonderful substance and these limpid colors of which we vainly seek the secret. I am very afraid that it will not be new theories that will reveal this secret to us" (Ambroise Vollard, *Renoir*, 1920).

Not even Cézanne escaped from this sort of preoccupation, and one can almost say that his entire life was no more than a struggle against the difficulty that he had in realizing materially those visions which he felt so powerfully. He told Emile Bernard: "What I lack is realization. Perhaps I will achieve it, but I am old and it is possible that I will die without having touched this supreme point: Realization! Like the Venetians" (*Souvenirs sur Paul Cézanne*, 1921).

This declaration is made even more moving by one which he made at the end of his life: "I am too old, I have not realized my idea, and I will not realize it now!"

The master of Aix, so powerfully unconventional, did not deny the need of craft and did not hide his admiration for that of the Venetians: "One must be a workman in one's art, one must know early

◁ *Small Italian Landscape
 seen through a Window, c. 1856-1857.
 Oil on canvas.*

▷ *The Rape of the Sabines
 (after Poussin), c. 1861-1863.
 Oil on canvas.*

on one's method of realization... The greatest, you know them better than I: the Venetians and the Spaniards." And further, speaking again of the Venetians: Your need to find a moral, intellectual support in those works which assuredly cannot be surpassed puts you perpetually on the alert, sets you on the ceaseless research of methods of interpretation that will certainly lead you to sense your methods of expression through nature." Or further: "These admirable works that have transmitted an age to us where we find a comfort, a support, as does the bather in the plank."

These words take on a curious interest, coming as they do from one whose goal was to "make his sensations concrete," to "express himself according to his personal temperament," to "regain the child's way of seeing."

As for Degas, at the end of his life the same subject (technique) became one of his chief concerns. However, in reality he had always been deeply preoccupied by it.

His youthful works are expertly executed but do not reveal any special interest in the sort of researches that preoccupied him later.

However, from this time forward, Degas seems to have had several motives for copying the old masters. He appears not only to have sought to ennoble his style and gain more facility in drawing and composition, but also to appropriate for himself the practice of a craft which he lacked as much as his contemporaries and immediate predecessors.

During his sojourns in Italy, Degas did copies after the Florentine primitives and the great masters of the sixteenth century, as evidenced by numerous drawings and copies in oil after Bellini and Titian.[1] But the most studied and elaborated copies that he did were executed in Paris at the Louvre where he made the acquaintance of Manet (1859), Fantin-Latour and Berthe Morisot. It was in this period that the preoccupation with craft grew in him and incited him to deepen his study of works that he admired. His copy of Poussin's *Rape of the Sabines*, the last in date and the most complete, is typical in this respect. Nonetheless, he had already previously copied the *Christ between the Two Thieves* of Mantegna, the portrait of Anne of Cleves by Holbein and the two heads of men of the Italian School.[2]

Uncertainty about technique continued to grow in Degas, and if it was only of secondary importance in his youth, it ended by slowly passing into the forefront of his thoughts. Georges Jeanniot wrote:

Often we would speak of craft, Degas, Chialiva and I, this craft which the old masters knew, thanks to which they could leave splendid works that stayed unchanged despite the passage of centuries. Degas appeared to think and all of a sudden said to us: "We live in a funny time, it must be admitted. This painting in oils that we do, this difficult craft that we practice without having a real command of it! A similar inconsistency has doubtless never existed. There were tried and true methods that the artists of the seventeenth and eighteenth centuries practiced; methods still known to David, a student of Vien, who was the dean of the Academy of Fine Arts, but the painters of the early nineteenth century were no longer acquainted with them" (*La Revue Universelle*, October 15 and November 1, 1933).

Since Degas had always felt the desire to rework his pictures in order to improve them, he would have had a particular need for a craft which would permit him to carry out later operations without spoiling the work he was retouching. Unfortunately, lacking a sure technique, he destroyed or disfigured many of his canvases.

The fate of Degas's portrait of *Mademoiselle Fiocre in the Ballet "La Source"* is well known.

Degas had sent this picture to the Salon, I no longer recall which year. On varnishing day, which at that time was no empty word, he looked at his picture anxiously, thinking that it was not very striking when hung. The painting was completely fresh since he had worked on it just the night before, and as a consequence it appeared cloudy and dull. He thus told the varnisher who was passing by with his brush and pot of varnish: "So! Go ahead! Give it a coat!" Whether or not the painting gained anything by this treatment I cannot say. In any case, as usual, when it returned to the studio it certainly did not please its creator who removed the varnish in order to rework the picture. Disaster! The removal of the varnish naturally removed half the painting as well. In order not to destroy the whole Degas was forced to leave his task unfinished. For years, the canvas stayed like that in a corner of the studio. It was only considerably later (between 1892 and 1895 I believe) that Degas found this picture again and took it into his head to work on it anew. He called in a restorer who removed the remaining varnish as well as he could and gave the necessary instructions for executing the retouches and repairing the damage done by Degas himself to his own painting. Degas was only half-satisfied with the result" (Ernest Rouart, *Degas*, 1937).

Mademoiselle Fiocre in the Ballet "La Source," c. 1866-1868. Oil on canvas.

For similar reasons a large number of unfinished canvases crowded his studio where they stayed until his death.

Thanks to the advice of his friend the painter Luigi Chialiva, who was particularly knowledgeable about different pictorial techniques, a small number of such pictures could be taken up again and completed. Examples are *The Rape* (Philadelphia Museum of Art, now called *Interior Scene*) and the *Woman with a Vase* from the Camondo Collection, where one can distinguish the retouches in the plant. Georges Jeanniot tells the story of the former canvas:

Degas introduced me to an Italian painter, a charming man, who knew everything there was to know about the craft of painting in oil. He had been frequenting copyists for many years, who, in the museums of Florence and Rome, spent their time reproducing the paintings of the masters. His name was Luigi Chialiva; a friend who was kind-hearted, always ready to help out, he gave me the best advice. Not only did he know the craft like an old master, but he saw at first glance what one should do to improve a picture. While putting his studio in order, Degas saw that a beautiful picture entitled *Interior Scene* had been deteriorated by humidity. What could be done?

"We must ask Chialiva."

Upon seeing the damage, Chialiva said: "This painting can be repaired, only certain precautions are necessary, because the ground has lifted from the canvas. In order to fix it will require some time. Once the ground is dry, I will show you how to set it in order to repaint the man's head. You can do it after the study that you used to paint your figure the first time."

This took a long time, but it was successful.

The picture repaired as if by a miracle, Degas, his palette in his hand, rose from his seat, and looking at Chialiva, said, "Well then! As it is, we will sell it for 100,000 francs!" And indeed, the picture brought that sum (*La Revue Universelle*, October 15 and November 1, 1933).

Without a doubt, of all the artists of the late nineteenth century, Degas is the one who was most disturbed by the question of craft. Although the manner of painting that he employed in his youth enabled him to produce works remarkable for their precision and tight drawing, he was not satisfied by his early technique and never ceased to investigate new methods of expression. This research lasted all his life, as a chronological study of his oeuvre would demonstrate. Unfortunately, such a study is inapplicable here because of the diversity of the procedures used by Degas: not one of these consistently corresponds to a period that can be neatly defined.

GLUE AND EGG TEMPERA

Degas was struck by the sober impact and matt appearance of Italian frescoes. Seeking to produce an analogous effect in his own work, he experimented with gouache and with glue and egg tempera.

Degas executed only a few paintings entirely in glue tempera due to the difficulties inherent in a medium that must be used warm. However, as we will see below, he apparently combined glue tempera with pastels.

The *Dancers Practicing at the Bar* in the Metropolitan Museum of Art, New York, is one of the paintings executed solely in glue tempera. Degas was content in this instance to follow the traditional and well-known method of mixing the hide glue and pigments over heat and keeping the mixture warm until the moment of putting paint to canvas. Thus, he did not bring any novelty to this method of painting.

His love of the Italian primitives naturally induced Degas to research their techniques and at one point he attempted to master egg tempera. However, instead of employing egg yolk as his medium he used only the egg white, which produced highly unreliable results. His painting cracked to the point of self-destruction. Discouraged, he abandoned this technique forever.

It seems undeniable that Degas believed he was following a standard procedure and that he neither sought to rediscover a lost technique nor endeavored to create a new one. One must conclude that he was capable of error in this regard.

And although surprising, his mistake can be explained. He must have read somewhere (or perhaps only have heard through word of mouth) that the early painters frequently made use of egg white. Degas probably confused the use of this medium with true egg tempera.

Indeed, the use of egg white is a recurrent theme in the early treatises on painting, both in the handbooks by Theophilus and Cennino Cennini and in an anonymous fourteenth-century study of illumination. Apparently illuminators made the most use of this medium. It served as a carrier for their pigments, as a component of the ground used for

Dancers Practicing at the Bar, c. 1876-1877. Glue tempera on canvas.

gilding, and especially to fix the gold to this ground. However, painters frequently gilded large areas of their panels using the same methods as the illuminators. Therefore they also utilized egg white. Moreover, in the chapter describing the method of preparing the ground to receive the gold, the author of the treatise on illumination clearly specifies that painters proceed in the same manner in their panels.[3]

It is also noteworthy that when Cennino Cennini discussed how one must prepare "the perfect tempera for gilding" with an egg white ("tempera" is used here in the most general meaning that it had) he is writing about painting and not about illumination. Indeed, his

explanation begins: "When you have finished the raised areas of your painting..."[4] Moreover, all of this section of his study deals with painting and not with illumination. To the latter he devotes other chapters in which, as expected, egg white is similarly prescribed for gilding.[5] Finally, it was not only for gilding that painters made use of egg white. Some pigments could not be used in gum, necessitating the use of egg white. As Theophilus wrote: "All these pigments and their differing hues can be ground and laid in with this gum except vermilion, white lead and carmine which must be ground and applied with the clear part of the egg."[6] This instruction concerned the painter on panel as well as the artist on paper or parchment.

Degas never studied the early treatises on painting and only knew these works through snatches heard or read here and there. Very probably he was ignorant of the distinctions between the different uses for egg white, and if he knew from some source that artists sometimes applied their pigments in egg white, he thought that this statement comprised true egg tempera painting.

It is very possible that Degas's "egg tempera" painting would have been less fragile if before its use the egg white had been strained through a sponge, as recommended in the treatise on illumination.[7] Degas assuredly used the egg white in its natural state.

It is surprising that Degas should be ignorant of these different treatises at a time when he was so eagerly researching a technique which could answer his requirements. But he always preferred personal experience and direct observation of the old masters to reference to the written word.

Singer with Glove, 1878. Pastel and tempera on canvas.

The Ballet, c. 1879. Pastel on silk. Fan painting.

GOUACHE

Degas sometimes retouched his pastels with gouache, but he used this medium consistently only for his fans. Although they number relatively few in his oeuvre, the fans merit mention for the rarity of their workmanship and for the charming effects which Degas could achieve with his technique.

Degas painted a few fans in his early youth. One of them is executed in pure watercolor over a drawing in ink and represents Spanish dancers accompanied by a guitarist who is said to be Alfred de Musset. At least, this is the story told by Berthe Morisot to whom the object was given by Degas himself. However, even though it must date from approximately the same period, another fan exhibits an entirely different facture: a large amount of gouache was used and the fan is worked in the smallest details. It also depicts Spanish dancers.

It is difficult to recognize Degas's hand in these works, although some of the dancers' movements already prefigure his future as a painter of the ballet.

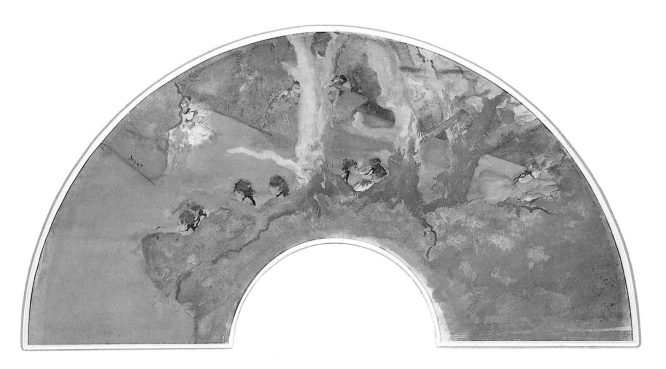

Dancers and Stage Scenery, c. 1879.
Gouache with gold highlights on silk. Fan painting.

One must look to a later period, probably 1875-1880, to find another series of fans which he executed in a totally different style and medium. When designing fans, Degas allowed himself to be carried away by the fantasy inherent in such objects. He was thereby able to produce unexpected decorative effects through the use of rare materials and precious craftsmanship that made masterpieces of these feminine playthings.

Drawn in gouache and watercolor, the costumes of the dancers were often heightened with gold and silver. Skirts of light gauze decorated with sequins were added as well. Executed in perfect taste, these details gave the ensemble an air of precious and refined work.

A few of these fan-shaped drawings were actually mounted and perhaps used by their owners at the expense of their freshness and impact. The sequins of gold and silver fell off, while the figures were erased by folding and unfolding.

The reliefs in precious metal on these fans denote a care for realism at the same time as a predilection for rich materials. But apart from these curious works, the use of gouache did not provoke Degas to attempt any original experiments.

"PEINTURE À L'ESSENCE" ON PAPER

A method which Degas used far more than tempera and gouache was "peinture à l'essence" on paper with de-oiled colors, that is, colors from which he leached the excess oil by putting them on blotting paper prior to using them.

It is important to make a careful distinction between works executed in this way and preliminary sketches for oil paintings which were done in colors only thinned with spirits, such as the *Two Amateurs*, the *Ballet Rehearsal on the Set*, or the *Woman Ironing*.

Ballet Rehearsal on the Set, 1874. Oil colors thinned with spirits on canvas.

Woman with Chrysanthemums, 1865. Peinture à l'essence on paper.

Furthermore, although Degas used "peinture à l'essence" on paper principally to sketch studies, he also produced entire paintings using this method which are filled with figures and very finished, such as the *Woman with Chrysanthemums*, the *Misfortunes of the City of Orleans*, *The Pedicure*, *The Beach*, *Women Grooming Themselves*, *In Front of the Grandstand*, and *Jockeys before the Race*.

Women Grooming Themselves, c. 1875-1876. Peinture à l'essence on oiled (?) paper.

▷ *The Pedicure, 1873. Peinture à l'essence on paper.*

It would be interesting to make the comparison between this last work and the equine scenes executed in casein by John Lewis Brown (1829-1890). It seems likely that Degas, who much admired Lewis Brown, sought to obtain an appearance analogous to that achieved by painting in casein.

Among the studies executed by Degas in "essence" on paper, the most important are the *Portrait of Giulia Bellelli*, a study for the portrait of the Bellelli family, the *Laundresses Carrying Laundry*, the *Woman Before a Window*, the *Horseman in Red*, the *Ballet Master*, and the *Young Woman Dressed for the City*.

The Misfortunes of the City of Orleans (Scene of War in the Middle Ages),
Salon of 1865. Peinture à l'essence on paper.

Since Degas was not yet thirty years old when he painted the Bellelli family portrait, he apparently had been employing this technique since his youth. Indeed, this painting cannot date after 1864, the year of Baron Bellelli's death, and most probably dates a few years before (P.A. Lemoisne assigns it to about 1860). Moreover, the *Woman with Chrysanthemums* and the *Misfortunes of the City of Orleans* are only slightly later since the first is dated 1865 and since the second appeared in the Salon of the same year.

Degas used the same method for numerous studies of dancers and jockeys, notably those executed on colored bristol, that constitute a true series to which must be linked the study of the *Ballet Master* already cited.

A *Portrait of a Man* and a study for *Lyda, the Woman with the Lorgnette* must also be added to the list of works in "essence."

The idea came to Degas to ally this method with oil. One finds a particularly interesting example of this work in a *Nude in the Bathtub* executed in "essence" on bristol tinted with de-oiled colors and retouched with oil years later.

Certain studies in "essence" in which much of the support remains uncovered unfortunately have been varnished. Under the effect of this treatment, the colored paper serving as a background has taken on a brownish tone which changes the original appearance of these works. The *Woman before a Window* is the most typical example of this harmful varnishing, of which so many paintings on cardboard by Toulouse-Lautrec have also been the victims. The *Laundresses Carrying Laundry*, although less damaged, has undergone the same treatment, as has a study of a young girl for *The Rape* and a small head of Achille de Gas. Evidently, this varnish is harmful only to the extent that the cardboard or tinted paper serving as background has remained uncovered. If the paintings cover their supports entirely, one need not fear that their natural tint has been modified and deepened.

The practice of "peinture à l'essence" executed in the above-described conditions, that is with colors leached of their oil and then applied to a paper support, is apparently unique to Degas. However, considered singly, not one of these characteristics, neither the use of paper as a support, nor the use of spirits, nor even the de-oiling of the colors, was a novelty.

Painting in oil on paper was quite ancient since the Reims museum possesses a number of studies of heads executed by Cranach, Holbein and Amberger from the Monthelon bequest. The flowing brushwork of these paintings proves that the paper must have been sized strongly enough so that the oil was not absorbed and so that the artist was permitted to let the colors lightly glide over the support surface.

The very pronounced "bistre" tone of these works derives without doubt from the varnish with which they were later covered.

The Louvre owns another early work in this technique: a head of a man on paper by Memling which appears to have been painted in oil.

Moreover, although he did not execute entire pictures using this technique, Rubens used pigments in oil to heighten Italian drawings done on paper in pen and ink and washes. Generally these drawings date from the period of the Italian decadence and were probably not of a style beautiful enough to suit his taste. Rubens therefore did not hesitate to "correct" them, which of course astonishes us. Being prepared for ink, the paper of these drawings was slightly sized.[8]

The use of paper as a support was apparently not lost during the seventeenth and eighteenth centuries because in a re-publication dated 1766 of a work by Roger de Piles one finds the following advice: "Those who lack these prepared papers or canvases could proceed in the following manner: take a somewhat strong sheet of paper, rub it with oil and paint on it at that very instant; this alternative to prepared papers will be found very pleasing" (*Eléments de peinture pratique*, 1766).

Laundresses Carrying Laundry, c. 1876-1878. Peinture à l'essence on paper.

In the nineteenth century many artists painted on rather thick, sized paper completely covered by a ground layer of oil paint. Almost all of Corot's studies of nature, those he did in Italy in particular, were so executed.

Indeed, this thick, prepared support is still widely used. It has the advantage of being easy to store and transport, but the inconvenience of becoming fragile and thus easily cracked due to the long-term effect of the oil "ground" on the paper. Degas sometimes used the commercially available bristol board and sometimes simply a lightly sized paper. Since this stock had not been specially prepared for painting in oil, it is totally different from the papers used by other nineteenth-century artists. In addition, Degas sometimes executed large works like the *Misfortunes of the City of Orleans* or the *Woman with Chrysanthemums* on a paper support. Other artists generally used paper only for studies.

Lastly and above all, Degas would use a paper support when painting with colors he had de-oiled. This de-oiling of the colors is the second and the most important part of the question.

The Italian masters were familiar with this procedure. It is known that paintings in oil executed in glazed and partially thinned pastes (*demi-pâtes*) on a solid support in monochrome or chiaroscuro was practiced in certain Italian schools during the Renaissance.

The first artist to have had the idea of systematically using this procedure seems to have been Leonardo da Vinci. After him the Venetians and Correggio used it according to their own peculiar genius.

In order to truly fulfill its role, the monochromatic sketch had to be reinforced with opaque colors. To this end the aforementioned painters used colors with good covering power which they furthermore de-oiled in order to obtain the high degree of opacity which an overly greasy and oily paste could not give them.

According to Luigi Chialiva, Leonardo de-greased his colors with spike lavender extract. It is highly probable that the artist used the chemical equipment seen by Pope Julius II to obtain this extract and not for the manufacture of varnish as the Pope believed.[9]

Chialiva also states that the desiccant that the Venetians used was turpentine or "aqua regia," while Correggio used naphtha rectified with sulphuric acid as described in the recipe given by M. de Saussure in the *Annals of Chemistry and Physics* of 1817.

This practice of de-oiling colors was lost, and Reynolds did not have recourse to it when he tried to imitate the system of matt and opaque underlayers used by the Italian masters. (He sought to obtain the same result by mixing varnishes with his colors, to be discussed below.)

Thus, if Degas reinstated a lost procedure, it was not he who had the initial idea. His innovation lies in the use that he made of it. The Venetians only used this method for their preparatory work which was destined to be covered with oil colors. Degas, on the other hand, executed entire works in this medium, and these retain a particular character quite special to this genre of painting.

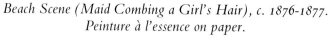

Beach Scene (Maid Combing a Girl's Hair), c. 1876-1877.
Peinture à l'essence on paper.

Woman Ironing, 1882. Oil colors thinned with spirits on paper.

PAINTINGS ON OILED PAPER

Certain works by Degas can be mistaken for paintings in varnish extracts. These are the preparatory works that he did on oiled paper.

The use of bristol for a support gave Degas a taste for slick surfaces, and he wanted to try another method of drawing with a brush on a smooth support. He rubbed a sheet of paper with oil and in this greasy and flowing material, with a fine, thin sable, he could draw his studied arabesques with virtuosity.

It is possible that he spontaneously devised this procedure without knowing that it had already been practiced. In any case, the recommendation of Roger de Piles cited above apropos the use of paper proves that it was not new.

Two Grooms on Horseback, 1875-1877. Peinture à l'essence on oiled paper.

The action of the oil unfortunately proved harmful for the paper that it covered, darkening it to such a degree that the works so executed are scarcely visible due to the overall brown tone of the paper. This effect is accentuated more and more with time, as can be seen by observing the *Two Grooms on Horseback*. The appearance is analogous to that caused by the varnishing of tinted paper, and it is often impossible to differentiate the two phenomena in photographs.

It is probably the darkening problem that prevented Degas from using oiled paper more frequently. Nonetheless, one finds it in a *Group of Women under Parasols* and for several studies of jockeys.

Horseman in Red, c. 1864-1868.
Peinture à l'essence on paper.

Madame Edmondo Morbilli (Thérèse de Gas, the Artist's Sister),
c. 1869. Pastel on paper.

PASTEL

It is undeniable that, out of his uncertainty and research for an ideal method, pastel emerged as the medium that best answered Degas's needs, or was at least the best suited to his experiments. The number of works and studies of all types executed in this medium is by far superior to what he was able to produce in oil, "essence," tempera or gouache.

Degas used pastel since his youth for small portraits of which the most complete and the most successful seems to be the portrait of his sister standing against a fireplace in a beige dress. This work is executed in a very detailed manner, without impasto and with smooth and even touch.

Various landscape studies which he completed before 1870 are done in the same technique, or at least exhibit a very similar facture. These are seascapes, shores and studies of the sky which constitute a special series that can be clearly differentiated from all the landscapes he would later do in pastel by their thin, blended medium lightly spread over the paper and their soft and shrouded tonality.

At this time Degas also used this procedure for preparatory studies of portraits executed in oils. For example, for the portrait of *Madame Camus at the Piano* he not only did preparatory drawings but four studies in pastel as well. One pastel represents the bust portrait of Madame Camus, another shows the young woman at the piano, a third is a study

Houses by the Sea, c. 1869. Pastel on paper.

of the arm and hand placed on the piano, and the fourth is a still life comprising the piano, the music and the mirror.

Similarly, for the oil portrait of *Madame Gobillard* done in 1869, he did a bust profile of his model in pastel, a study so worked that in itself it constitutes a complete and finished picture.

Nonetheless, pastel was still at this time only an ancillary method of production for Degas and oil painting evidently remained his primary preoccupation. He even seems to have abandoned pastel for several years. It is possible that his voyage to America was the cause of pastel's momentary disgrace. But, doubtless unhappy with oil painting and what it gave him as a product, it was not long before Degas returned to the use of pastel.

Madame Camus at the Piano, 1869. Oil on canvas.

No pastels survive from the years immediately following Degas's sojourn in the United States, but one cannot thereby conclude that the artist produced nothing in pastel during this period since Degas only rarely dated his works. Of course, neither can one determine the precise moment that Degas renewed his interest in the colored crayon, but in any case the renunciation of pastel could not have lasted more than a few years, given the large number of works executed in this medium between his return to France in 1873 and 1885.

In many pastels by Degas his chosen subjects are made into abstractions through his way of conceiving them and the originality of his composition. However, he scarcely deviates from the common technique for the use of this medium.

Pastels like *The Star*, the *Woman Crouching in her Tub*, *In the Wings*, the *Lowering of the Curtain*, *The Loge*, *The Harlequin*, the *Woman in the Tub*, the *Reclining Bather*, and the *Woman at her Toilette* do not exhibit any peculiarities of technique, which is indeed classic.

However, in other works Degas is already seeking to vary the appearance of the medium through the use of new methods devised by himself, and to break the uniformity of the execution by using in one picture techniques borrowed from many different procedures. It is in this way that he mixes pastel, gouache, tempera and very probably "peinture à l'essence" as well.

The careful study of a few specimens of this mixed series gives us precious information.

◁ *Woman Crouching in her Tub, 1886. Pastel on cardboard.*

▷ *In the Wings, 1882-1885. Pastel.*

Upon first examination of the *Dancers behind a Stage Set* one can easily perceive that if the skin, hair and skirts of the dancers are rendered in "classic" pastel, the greenery decorating the set in the right background, the flowers ornamenting the coiffures, the back of the stage set, the floor of the stage, and the leg of the dancer in the immediate foreground are executed in brush by a method of painting which is thin but wet. This medium could be gouache, tempera, "peinture à l'essence" or pastel diluted with water. A more detailed examination reveals that Degas did not use the same procedure for the stage floor, for example, as for the scene decoration in the background. Indeed, for the back of the stage set and for the stage floor, both of which are executed in the same manner, it seems almost certain that we have an example of pastel applied in water with a brush, which gives it the thin and transparent appearance of a wash. It is an entirely different question in the greenery of the set decoration. This detail presents matt impastos which can only result from tempera or gouache. The flowers decorating the hair of the central dancer are undeniably due to the same procedure (that is, most probably tempera), even though they exhibit less impasto than the greenery decorating the set and reveal neither the touch of the artist nor obvious brushwork.

The *Ballet of "L'Africaine"* presents another passage of mixed media which is very different from the one discussed above. At first sight one can discern that the entire background of the picture, which represents a stage set of mountains, trees and sky, is painted with a brush, while in the foreground the figures and the necks of the cellos are executed in pastel crayon. Examining the background, one could almost be convinced that neither tempera nor gouache were used here but rather "peinture à l'essence." Further examination indicates that the foreground areas that have been reinforced with pastel probably cover an underlayer painted in the same manner as the background. Although one cannot be absolutely certain, the above observations lead one to conclude that the entire work was first painted in "essence" and while the background was left in its first state, the foreground was retouched in pastel.

Dancers behind a Stage Set, c. 1880. Pastel and tempera on paper.

Dancer with Bouquet, End of the Arabesque, 1876-1877. Tempera and pastel on canvas.

◁ *Dancer with a Bouquet Bowing on the Stage, 1878. Pastel on paper.*

The two versions of *Dancer with a Bouquet* from the Camondo Collection are also combinations of pastel and brushwork, but their technique is nonetheless very different. The *Dancer with a Bouquet Bowing on the Stage* is for the most part done in pastel crayon with only a few areas painted with a brush. On the other hand, the *Dancer with a Bouquet, End of the Arabesque* exhibits far more work in brush than in pastel.

In the former, only the dancer's leg and foot are clearly executed in a wet medium. Other areas seem treated in the same manner, but in a less obvious way, such as in the bouquet and notably in the paper that envelops it; on the stage; and perhaps also in the scenery. There are no impastos such as one sees in the *Dancers behind a Stage Set*, and it seems that Degas has simply spread the pastel with water, unless he has employed gouache here in a very delicate manner.

The *Dancer with Bouquet, End of the Arabesque* has a completely different technique and appearance. Despite the extreme mattness of the material employed and the delicacy with which the color has been applied in certain spots, despite these characteristics which make a brushstroke and a pastel highlight so closely resemble each other that they can be confused, this work has even more than the first an air of being painted. This is due to the fact that it was entirely covered by brushwork, even where pastel had been applied. It seems almost certain that in a first stage, Degas had painted his work in brush, then in a second stage highlighted it with pastel, and finally in a last stage redid a few areas very lightly in the initial medium. It is impossible to be certain whether the paint is gouache, tempera or "peinture à l'essence." However, it seems unlikely that "peinture à l'essence" could be de-oiled to the point that it would appear matt and would not cause any trace of ringing when brushed over the pastel layer. This is why this work must be executed in tempera or gouache. Between these two possibilities, tempera seems to be the most probable for the following reasons. In order to execute this layered work, Degas must have been obliged to add a large enough amount of glue or gum to the medium to maintain each layer's integrity. A large proportion of gum makes gouache less matt, but this is not true of tempera, which remains matt despite a strong dose of medium.

The *Dog Song* is another example of this composite medium. It too was probably first executed in pastel, then retouched later almost entirely in brush. Thus, a layer of paint covers the pastel almost completely, producing yet another technique that is slightly different from those already discussed. Furthermore, the brushwork is plainly visible even in the reproduction, and one can see that the picture does not have the appearance of pastel.

The Dog Song (At the Café-Concert), 1875-1877. Pastel and tempera.

Degas used yet another original procedure when researching methods to vary a medium. After sketching his subject in pastel, he blew boiling water over this drawing. He thus made the dusting of color into a paste and worked in this paste with brushes of varying stiffness. If the water had vaporized on thinly applied areas he obtained a wash that he spread with his brush. Naturally he was careful not to project the water vapor over the entire picture but rather reserved the original pastel in some places, which gave him a different facture for the various elements creating his work. The flesh of one dancer was not treated in the same manner as her tutu, and the scenery was of a different substance than the stage floor. The result is thus analogous to that obtained by the

◁ *The Star*
or Dancer on the Stage,
c. 1876-1877.
Pastel over monotype.

▷ *Dancer with a Fan,*
c. 1879.
Pastel moistened with steam.

procedures described previously, and once again produces a mixture of work in brush and pastel crayon.

The *Dancer with a Fan* is characteristic of this singular method, and if untrained eyes are not struck by it at first sight, an attentive examination of the work clearly reveals the use of moisture. For example, in the field one can still see the ridges made by the boiling water, and on the legs as well as on the belt of blue ribbon one recognizes the flatness of a color spread by water.

A mixture of work in brush and pastel is also found in *Ludovic Halévy and Albert Boulanger-Cavé in the Wings at the Opera (Portraits of Friends on the Stage)*, in a *Dancer with a Bouquet*, in a *Resting Dancer*, and in a group of *Three Dancers*.

◁ *Dancer with a Fan (detail),*
  c. 1879.
  Pastel moistened with steam.

▷ *Ludovic Halévy and*
  Albert Boulanger-Cavé
  in the Wings
  at the Opera, 1878-1879.
  Pastel and tempera on paper.

This diversity in the technique used for one picture has troubled art historians and the compilers of catalogues who do not know in which genre to class the described piece. One must avow that the difficulty is great and that to escape the situation one is often obliged to designate as "pastel" a work in which many other procedures have been utilized. This classification thus cannot be rigorous when discussing the oeuvre of Degas and must be used only as an expedient, that is as a way to more easily distinguish a picture from the whole of his production.

Whether by moistening the pastel or by introducing in the execution of the work another medium such as tempera or gouache, Degas seems to be the first to have combined drawing and painting in this way.

It is probable that pastel was used quite frequently by artists to correct oil paintings. However, in that case the pastelwork is only a provisional retouch used to judge the suitability of any modifications before they are rendered definitively and irreparably in oil. The character of these pastel studies is therefore essentially different from that of the mixed-media studies discussed in the preceding pages. The latter were not only intended to be definitive, but beyond that were purposefully designed by Degas for the realization of certain effects obtainable only from this diversity of materials.

Neither the careful examination of the oeuvre of earlier pastel artists nor the perusal of their notes permit the assumption that they created such works or shared Degas's intentions.

As for the method of moistening the pastel by blowing the vapor from boiling water over it, the merit of the invention incontestably belongs to Degas.

However novel Degas's methods, one cannot help but remark that the idea of using several different media in the execution of one work had been a general practice for centuries.

It had been common to retouch frescoes in tempera. After a fairly short time, the surface covering of fresco sets and it is impossible to continue the work in the same manner. It was thus necessary to have recourse to a second method of painting, of which the appearance did

Half-Length Dancers, 1899. Pastel.

not differ markedly from that obtained by the first. Tempera suggested itself.

It seems more unusual to us to place certain tones in gouache on a canvas already painted in oil. However, according to Boschini, it was in just this manner that Veronese was accustomed to paint his blues. The biographer adds that it is for this reason that imprudent persons have unwittingly effaced some areas of the master's paintings when cleaning them.[10]

According to the seventeenth-century manuscript of Sir Theodore Turquet de Mayerne, Van Dyck proceeded in the same fashion, laying down blues and greens with gum in water, and varnishing them once dry.

This custom is explained by the fact that blue was extracted from lapis or copper. Lapis was very expensive, and the color from copper was used more often. When mixed with oil, copper blues and their derivatives change color, altering the tones with which they are combined as well. However, when they are ground in gum and placed on an oil painting or on a part of an unpainted canvas, they are prevented from corroding themselves and their neighbors. The blues used today are not derived from copper and can be prepared in oil without danger.

If today restorers use tempera for retouching old paintings, it is for yet another reason. Tempera dries much more speedily than oil paint. The restorer thus sees the result of his work very quickly and the retouching has much less chance of being in disunity with the rest of the picture with time. A retouch in oil, on the other hand, would be modified over the course of years.

In the instances of combined media discussed above, it is always a matter of liquid colors applied with a brush. A very clear difference thus exists between such procedures and the completed works by Degas.

After 1880, perhaps already because of his failing vision, Degas seems to have abandoned this type of experiment in order to execute his pastels in a broader manner, with more obvious hatching and a richer color scheme.

Although he had always been careful to capture harmonious nuances and delicate tones, it seems that beginning in the eighties Degas wanted to obtain a greater richness and impact. Color increasingly became his preoccupation, although it did not cause him to neglect drawing, his great strength and constant passion.

Although in this period he has not yet arrived at the richness and power of color scheme seen in his pastels of about 1892-1895, Degas was already seeking methods that would make the color show to its best advantage. He forced it to strike the viewer more vividly and to proffer more rich and varied effects by using stronger contrasts, more pronounced reflections in flesh, and the most vivid tones in costumes.

In earlier periods Degas had taken care to mix the hatchings that created his design, but in the eighties he did not deepen and mix the

The Conversation, c. 1889-1890. Pastel.

colors. Instead, he juxtaposed opposing and contiguous colors, boldly bringing out the contrasts or concordances of their tones and values. This technique differs from those to be discussed below.

A number of works may be cited as examples of this manner: the *Dancer in Blue*, the *Toilette*, the *Coiffure after the Bath*, another *Toilette*, the *Woman in the Tub*, *Seated Woman*, a *Woman Sponging her Back*, a *Leaving the Bath*, two *Conversations*, *Before the Mirror*, another *Leaving the Bath*, *After the Bath*, *Stooping Woman Drying her Feet*, *At the Races, before the Start*, and the *Portrait of Zaccharian*.

◁ *After the Bath, 1883. Pastel.*

Seated Dancer Tying her Slipper, 1886. Pastel.

Leaving the Bath, 1885.
Pastel.

While allowing for the differences between oil painting and pastelwork, the technique described here may be compared to that of the Impressionists, particularly to that employed by Monet in his landscapes. In both cases the integrity of the individual strokes is maintained.

In general, one can say that Degas and the Impressionists used the contrast of opposition, unlike the old masters who principally used the contrast of saturation. It is well known that the appearance of a tone is modified by its environment. However, artists can use this truth in different ways. For example, while the Impressionists and the Neo-Impressionists exploited the emphasis obtainable for a color by placing it near its complementary, the old masters enlivened their colors by the juxtaposition of varying degrees of saturation of the same color.

For example, if after having established a graded palette and chosen a blue tone one juxtaposes the most attenuated part of this tone and its most intense part, the latter is reinforced while the former appears muted. However, to achieve this effect requires a knowledge of the old masters' methods and their unequaled mastery of technique. Brushing glazes or partially diluted pastes on canvases which had already received a special type of underpainting, the old masters obtained effects which modern painters cannot hope to achieve due to their lack of knowledge of the long lost sequence of these procedures.

Hatching has always been more or less employed in pastelwork but when these strokes are placed very close together the artist usually blends them with one another. Chardin is perhaps the first to leave the hatchings visibly discrete, as can be seen in the two self-portraits and the *Portrait of Madame Chardin*. Although Degas's contemporaries thus had a precedent for obvious hatchwork, it was not the custom then as it is now. Moreover, Degas not only left his pastel strokes discrete, but exaggerated this practice, pushing it to an extreme. His strokes became true stripes of grand dimensions, making his image incomprehensible when viewed at a short distance and necessitating a great viewing distance in order to obtain a good reading.

After the Bath, Woman Drying her Neck, 1898. Pastel on cardboard.

Woman Combing her Hair,
c. 1887-1890.
Pastel on paper.

Toward the years 1892-1895 Degas was haunted by the craftsmanship of the old masters which seemed perfect to him and which he was
very eager to achieve in the execution of his own works. As a consequence, he tried to approach their accomplishments through a new
and more informed technique for the use of pastels.

Not wanting to content himself with a painting in which only the
surface played a part and not seeking to render desired effects only by
direct oppositions of tones and values, he devised a way to make the
superimposed layers of color act upon each other and thereby hopefully
attain the magnificent results achieved by the Venetian methods, or at
least come as near to them as he could.

After the Bath (Nude Drying Herself), c. 1890. Pastel.

Degas sketched his painting with colors that were already very rich and pure, and thoroughly fixed this first layer. Then he could work anew on this colored surface without fearing that his pastels would raise the tones already laid down. Allowing the underlayer to show through in certain areas, he made the new tints act on this background, thereby neutralizing some colors and reinforcing others. He repeated this operation of fixing and placing the colors many times until the completion of the painting, that is until a point at which he felt satisfied with the work, a point, as one knows, he decided upon with difficulty.

In the years that followed he perfected this technique further, for which he continued to use non-smudged hatchwork. To this method we

Woman Leaving the Bath, 1895-1898. Pastel.

Three Russian Dancers, c. 1895. Pastel.

owe a magnificent series of dancers and nudes which are remarkable for their coloristic impact. Among the most typical of these works must be cited the *Half-Length Dancers*, done in 1899, *Dancers in the Wings*, the two *Resting Dancers*, *Green Dancers Resting*, the *Three Dancers*, the *Dancers coming on Stage*, a *Seated Dancer*, *After the Bath*, *Woman Drying her Neck*, the *Two Dancers in Pink and Yellow*, several *Russian Dancers*, a *Leaving the Bath*, a *Nude Drying Herself*, and an *After the Bath*.

Toward the end of the century Degas began to use tracings when making drawings and pastels. The chapter on drawing records the details of this procedure.

Degas unquestionably invented this application of successive layers of pastel in which each one is fixed before it is covered with the next. Apparently it occurred to him that pastel could be adapted to serve a technique in which different colors act upon each other by superposition and transparency as much as by the opposition of juxtaposed tones. Since the requisite transparency is not inherent to the pastel medium as it is to oil paint used in glazes, Degas could only produce an analogous effect by not entirely covering the underlayers, thereby leaving some openings through which the underlayer could be seen.

Racehorses, 1883-1885. Pastel on tracing paper.

Dancers with Yellow Skirts, 1903. Pastel.

The greatest difficulty posed by this technique is not to spoil the underlayers. A fixative of the first order is required, and Degas, after having tried a number of them only to find them unsatisfactory, was greatly assisted in this search by Luigi Chialiva. The idea for this technique was nonetheless conceived by Degas alone.

Portrait of a Young Woman, 1867. Oil on canvas.

OIL PAINTING

If Degas produced a greater number of pastels than of oil paintings, the main reason for this must be seen in his use of pastel to carry out the research and experiments to which he dedicated himself so actively in the second half of his life. Moreover, it must not be forgotten that he required much less time to finish even a very complex pastel than to bring a work executed in oil to the same degree of finish.

It cannot be denied that in his youth oil painting held first place for Degas. This part of his work is clearly differentiated from the rest. It consists of a series of portraits which are surprising for the rigorousness of their drawing and the meticulousness of their execution.

The influence of Ingres is undeniable and especially in Degas's early period makes itself evident in canvases like the *Self-Portrait in Half-Length,* the portrait of his sister *Madame Edmondo Morbilli,* or that of his brother *Achille de Gas as a Midshipman.*

Nevertheless, a tendency which will slowly turn Degas away from this model surfaces very early in his career. In fact, the desire to capture reality more closely, a desire which will become more and more pronounced in him, is already apparent in *The Bassoon, Pagans Singing and the Artist's Father, The Cellist Pillet,* or in the portraits of *Madame Camus at the Piano,* of *Mademoiselle Dubourg* and of *Hortense Valpinçon.* In works such as these, Degas seeks to locate his models in their natural

The Orchestra at the Opera, c. 1868-1869. Oil on canvas.

setting and to give them familiar poses. To the influence of Ingres is added that of the Dutch masters.

It was not long before a technical evolution parallel to this conceptual evolution modified Degas's execution of his new ideas. As his desire to make his portraits real scenes where the characters live rather than pose grew stronger, the paint medium became richer and the execution freer.

Nevertheless, the *Cotton Office in New Orleans*, dated 1873, which by its arrangement on the canvas (rather unexpected for the period) foresees a new manner of conceiving the composition and enlivening the movement of a painting, is still much closer to earlier works in its manner of execution. The *Woman with a Vase* dated 1872 is also very close to the portraits executed before 1870. But the *Woman Arranging a Bouquet*, which certainly was also conceived in New Orleans, reveals a much freer execution, although it is still painted in a technique which is rather smooth and without thick impasto.

The Cotton Office in New Orleans, 1873. Oil on canvas.

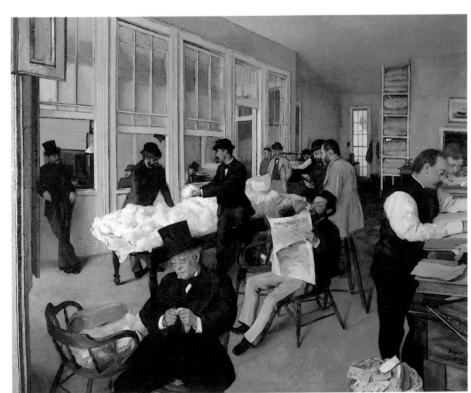

Madame Jeantaud Looking in the Mirror, c. 1875. Oil on canvas.

It is especially toward 1875 that the impasto becomes richer and thicker. And if in the *Portrait of Jeantaud, Linet and Lainé*, painted in 1871, the impasto is still quite thin, the portraits of *Madame Jeantaud Looking in the Mirror*, of *Henri Rouart in a Top Hat* in front of his factory dating from 1875, and of *Ernest May at the Bourse* painted between 1875 and 1880, are clearly more loaded with paint and richer in medium.

However, in spite of the characteristics which differentiate the Ingres-like portraits from those last cited, it is certain that all these paintings are still very far from those Degas will attempt to execute after or even during his experiments with pastel. He seemed to feel, at that time, that his technical mastery was not yet thorough enough to give him the sureness of hand he needed to express himself as he wished.

If it weren't Degas who was under consideration, such demands on oneself would be surprising. However, one must recognize that in spite of their very great merit and the great talent they exhibit, those portraits and little genre paintings which are akin to the paintings of the Dutch masters both in execution and in inspiration do not equal their models from a strictly technical viewpoint nor in the quality of the paintwork. Of course, only craftsmanship is being discussed here. One cannot deny the artistic value of these works in which this great artist could not escape introducing a style of rare grandeur and an observation of life which one rarely meets in so perceptive a form.

Children on the Doorstep of a House in New Orleans, 1873. Oil on canvas.

Portrait of Edmond Duranty, 1879. Tempera and pastel.

In any case, it is clear that the craftsmanship which served him to paint these undeniably successful works did not fully satisfy him because he abandoned it to research other technical means of execution.

From then on oil painting lost its position of prominence, henceforth occupied by pastel. This is the period of the daring and original experiments that Degas adored, such as the mixing of techniques or the use of large hatchings in strongly contrasting colors. Nevertheless his research and his successes in pastel did not make the artist completely forget oil painting, to which he had recourse from time to time. Interesting examples of what he then produced in oil are provided by the two portraits of *Diego Martelli* and that of *Madame Marin*. Even in its

Portrait of Diego Martelli, 1879. Oil on canvas.

present unfinished state the latter already shows a masterly conception and a richness of color which Degas hadn't previously achieved.

These latter canvases clearly reflect the influences of his work in pastel. Their broader conception, their much freer execution, their much more daring use of color strongly differentiate them from the paintings made before.

Although these developments are new, they are not unique to Degas but widespread at the time. One finds them in Manet, in Cézanne and in Monet as one will find them a little later in Van Gogh and Gauguin. It remains true, however, that Degas achieved this evolution through pastel. One could interpret his use of pastel simply as the accident of circumstances and consider it a question of time alone that made pastel and the new trends coincide. But it seems more correct to establish a rapport between the new medium and the new concepts without, however, being able to say which caused the other. It is certain that Degas allowed himself to be more daring and more free with pastel, which he felt he had mastered more than oil painting. But it is difficult to decide if it is the use of pastel which brings forth new aspirations in him or if new aspirations made him decide on the adoption of pastel. Whatever is the case, it is undeniable that this medium facilitated the blossoming of his new ideas.

The essential difference between the two procedures makes an identity of execution in oil painting and pastels impossible. But beyond the strength of the coloring and the breadth of the technique, the broad surfaces and the frank opposition of the tones used confer some common characteristics on the works in pastel and in oil executed by Degas during this period.

Nevertheless, even if he uses freely placed hatchings in his oil paintings, he can't generalize this habit as he does in pastel, especially not in the flesh tones of oil paintings where it would be detrimental to modelling. With his concern for precise form and modelling, he can't systematize this manner of painting as the Impressionists did. Rather, he most often uses tones in broad surfaces, a procedure one finds in Manet,

The Ballet Rehearsal,
c. 1875.
Gouache and pastel
over monotype.

Cézanne and Gauguin. But much more than Manet and especially more than Gauguin, he maintains an interest in three-dimensional relief.

In the previously mentioned portraits of *Diego Martelli* and *Madame Marin*, which aren't completely finished, one can partly distinguish his method of proceeding. The drawing of the faces is seen to be strongly re-enforced by an overlying line and waiting, it almost seems, for further work, a practice he used concurrently in pastel where it is natural. Certainly this brush-drawn line can be found in other artists, particularly Cézanne, Van Gogh and Gauguin. But among these artists there exist great differences in the execution of this line and in its desired purpose.

For Van Gogh and even more for Gauguin the line remains freely and definitively visible to accent and underline arabesques with an expressive and also in Gauguin's work with a decorative intent. With Cézanne its purpose is possibly to redefine the drawing which has been partly lost in the process of carrying out the work.

As for Degas, he usually proceeded as follows. When he found the curve of an arm or the movement of a leg defective, he went away from the canvas and made a drawing on paper, usually in charcoal, of the part with which he wasn't satisfied. Then he corrected his canvas from this drawing by using a painted line to redo the fragment in question. This correction wasn't done until the painting in process was dry and had to dry in turn itself before work was begun again. Examples of this working method are the *Ballet Rehearsal* and the *Four Dancers on Stage*.

In these latter paintings as well as in the three preceding portraits, one can see the brushed line because Degas had the intention of repainting these pictures and didn't consider them completely finished. It is certain that he didn't intend to leave the lines visible.

Another technique of painting which Degas will use later can be seen germinating in the canvases of this period. Instead of applying the underpainting and spreading the paint with a brush, he placed his tones with his thumb in large dabs which he thinned down and blended as necessary while working. This practice is very visible in some of his paintings. It recalls somewhat the use of hatchings in pastel, which is without doubt the reason why Degas adopted it so readily.

This technique can be clearly distinguished in the *Blue Dancers* where it so felicitously helps the colors interact and sing among themselves in a rare and delicate harmony, and in several other canvases such as *The Bath, Three Yellow Dancers*, another *Bath*, and *After the Bath* as well as the *Dancer Adjusting the Epaulette of her Corsage*. But with his need for precise form and his concern for the beautiful arabesque curves of drawing, he couldn't prevent himself—and it was necessary in a work so executed —from indicating the contours with a sable brush either fine for one line, or rich or diluted for others, which express so well the contour of a leg partly bent or the rounded curve of an arm.

It is certain that this way of applying paint to canvas isn't unique to Degas. It must occur to painters rather often to use their fingers to soften a passage, crush an impasto or apply a touch of color in one judiciously chosen place as in earlier times one placed a beauty-spot on a face.

Blue Dancers, c. 1890. Oil on canvas.

Dancers Mounting Stairs to the Stage, c. 1886-1890. Oil on canvas.

In her treatise on painting, Mrs Merrifield says that Titian frequently applied paint with his fingers, especially in the flesh tones. When there were large surfaces to glaze, he worked with all his fingers or with the flat of his hand. In this way he obscured the grooves left by his brush. For the delicate nuance of the flesh, he dipped one finger only into the paint and passed it over the canvas, rubbing lightly.[11]

Boschini also says that Titian enjoyed blending his last touches with his fingers.[12]

But if Titian occasionally used his fingers, and he isn't the only one, it certainly appears that Degas was the first to make a much more systematic use of them to execute the underpainting on his canvas. This technique gave him an underdrawing which has the advantage of presenting a surface to which the next paint layers adhere perfectly. This method also permits him to flatten the paint well and to at once avoid uneven impasto as well as grooves left by the brush.

It will be seen that Degas used this manner to apply the underpaint to the principal canvases which he carried out in the last years of his life.

The Ballet Rehearsal, c. 1891. Oil on canvas.

Occasionally Degas even continued this system through to the completion of the painting, as one can perceive upon examining the *Blue Dancers* cited above. This work is almost entirely carried out by means of dabs of paint lightly placed with a finger; only one line of the brush, thin, nimble and vigorous, indicates the contours of the figures.

One can distinguish nearly the same technique in the landscapes Degas made towards the end of his life when visiting his friend Braquaval at Saint-Valéry-sur-Somme. However, the technique of these works is more impasted and thicker since Degas was not able to prevent himself from reworking them from one year to the next during the different visits he made to his friend. As a result, certain ones have possibly been repainted over a period of several years.

The colors which he applied with his thumb were most often prepared in advance. Indeed, he extolled the virtues of this practice to the young painters whom he occasionally advised, a practice to which he turned even more willingly as he found in it some analogy with pastel: in both methods the tints must be prepared in advance and are not composed by the artist himself at the moment in which he puts the colors on canvas or on paper.

It was during this period that Degas had his maidservant Zoé read to him the *Journal* of Delacroix, and he often spoke of it with his painter friends.

The lists of Delacroix's different palettes excited Degas tremendously. He had been able to obtain some of them from the atelier of the master where samples of the tones were carefully placed one after the other in a scientific order. Next to each tone was written a list of the elements of which they were constituted.

But the complexity of the mixtures prepared by Delacroix for his different compositions, which were necessary to him especially when he had his students help him, could not be useful to Degas, at least not to the same degree. The latter evidently used more simplified ranges of colors which he conceived during the course of his work or at least at the beginning of each session.

Therein lies a rather important pictorial problem. If some artists like to have their colors prepared in advance, others prefer to compose them on their palette according to their need as they proceed. That is the most common procedure, but some schools, such as the Impressionists and the Neo-Impressionists, have claimed that they no longer mix the colors themselves, neither on the palette nor even on the canvas. They placed only small strokes of pure color on the canvas which, juxtaposed, were to mix themselves on the retina of the observer standing at a certain distance. "He makes no or almost no mixtures of tones on the palette, which is covered only with little commas of nearly pure color," says Albert André of Renoir.

The custom of preparing the tones in advance was taken from fresco and tempera painting, where the use of liquid colors which dried relatively quickly obliged the artist to keep them in containers and did not permit him to combine them on the palette. Too liquid at first to stick to the palette, initially they would have flowed, only to be too solidified to use a short time later. It was therefore necessary to have recourse to containers not only for the basic colors but even for the mixtures. It was for this reason that Cennino Cennini describes the compositions of different hues for coloring faces or clothing in fresco or in tempera and why he advises having as many containers as there are nuances, from the highlights of those surfaces in relief to the shadows of hollows.[13]

Even though the necessity for premixing disappears with the arrival of oil painting, apparently the great Italian masters of the sixteenth century generally continued this practice of preparing all the tones ahead of time. For example, we find in Lomazzo's treatise entire pages enumerating precisely all the different amounts necessary to create a range of different tones. After giving recipes which one must follow to obtain the flesh tint of a bilious person, of a sanguine, of a lymphatic and of a melancholy person, he proceeds to divide these tonalities into six gradations, three for the bright, highlighted part, and three for the shaded part. Moreover, the composition of not a single one of the combinations corresponding to these different degrees is omitted. Further on, Lomazzo describes in the same detailed and precise manner methods for coloring the parts of a drapery red, blue, green or yellow.[14]

This procedure was probably followed by the northern schools as well because the manuscript of Sir Theodore Turquet de Mayerne also contains lists of the tones which had to be combined in order to paint flesh, hair, drapery, satin, velvet, leaves, the sea, the sky, fire and metals.[15] Nonetheless, Mayerne doesn't match Lomazzo's precision and he leaves to the painter the burden as well as the freedom of improvising mixtures of colors according to the nuances which he observes in the model or the motif.

Neither did the French artists renounce this ancient procedure, which was recommended by Roger de Piles in his compendium of the elements of practical painting. According to him, before starting to paint it is necessary to mix all the colors which one will need on the palette with a palette knife. He even gives a diagram of this palette, showing the order in which the colors should be arranged on it.[16]

Delacroix, who had to carry out large-scale decorations at numerous periods of his life, generalized the use of prepared colors in a way that suited his purposes and did so very systematically and methodically. For each of these paintings he carefully set in order an appropriate palette, the composition of which he then remembered by placing little samples of each of the prepared tints on a large sheet of paper. He wrote beside each little spot of color the list of its components.

Degas enthusiastically acquired some of these paper palettes, and it was with an intense pleasure that he found in Delacroix's *Journal* the lists of the colors used for certain canvases or figures.[17]

Delacroix numbered his colors, and as a result, he could indicate in a precise manner to his assistants the nuances they should place in each area. One day Andrieu, wanting to test him, put pink no. 3 where his master had told him to put pink no. 2. But Delacroix, even though he was on the floor and the area in question was on the ceiling, protested immediately. It was not only in his large decorative compositions that Delacroix proceeded in this manner. One can also find in his diary lists of colors which were meant for easel paintings.

As for Degas, he was certainly not forced into using such a method because of the practical requirements of the material involved as is the case with fresco, tempera, or even with monumental decorations executed by helpers. It is from the pictorial viewpoint itself that he found real advantages in this system.

The very happy results which he obtained from pastel by the superposition of tones successively fixed on paper impelled him around 1895 to attempt to achieve analogous effects with oil paint.

It was during this period and under the sway of his special concerns with old techniques that one series of nude women at their toilettes was painted, of which the most characteristic are a *Nude Woman Drying Herself*, a *Woman Leaving the Bath*, and a *Woman Drying Herself*.

He carried out his underpainting in monochrome with his thumb in the manner already described. He has left a canvas at this stage. It is a

The Bath, 1890. Oil on canvas.

Nude Woman Drying Herself, which allows us to know the appearance of one of his works in the process of its construction. It is, therefore, precious for the study of the pictorial techniques practiced by Degas.

After having let this underpainting dry, he covered it with copal varnish dissolved in oil by rubbing the copal on by hand. He continued work on the slippery surface thus obtained. At that point, he counted on painting only with glazes and scumbles. But dissatisfied with the results achieved in this manner, when executing a work he usually couldn't prevent himself from continuing an opaque application that tended towards true impasto, contrary to his initial plan.

When he felt the urge to retouch old canvases like *The Rape* or the *Portrait of the Painter James Tissot*, he likewise rubbed the parts to be repainted with copal in oil. This technique of rubbing an oily substance onto a painted surface which one plans to rework is an old practice. Actually, in his *De' veri precetti della pittura* (1587), Armenini already mentions it. After having explained that one paints by glazing on the finished and well-dried underpainting, he says: "To facilitate the execution, it is necessary first to coat the part which one will repaint by rubbing it with fingers dipped in clarified walnut oil. One spreads this oil very evenly with the palm of the hand, then one wipes it with a clean cloth, because, if one hasn't removed it, the colors yellow with time. This preparation much facilitates the work, in that the tones blend and can be applied without the lower layers rejecting them, so that the most difficult things can be carried out with no trouble."[18]

Degas's obsession with the craftsmanship of the old masters became stronger and stronger. This is clear from an experience of 1897, related by a student:

When Degas had me copy the Mantegna of the Louvre, *Wisdom Victorious over the Vices*, he had new ideas about the techniques of the ancients and had me carry out this copy following a technique conceived by him which recalled that of the Venetians more than that of Mantegna. In sum, he wanted to experiment with processes which he had pictured in his fertile imagination in diverse combinations, but the actual practical implementation of which he wasn't certain. I perceived this clearly during the execution. He told me first: "You will prime the canvas for me in green. It will be left to dry for months outside. Titian waited maybe for a year before continuing to work on a painting. Then, on this well-dried underpainting we will glaze in red, and we will have the desired tone."

I apply my underpainting in green earth. Degas comes to see me at the Louvre: "But that isn't green, that's gray! Do it for me in apple green!" I then take up the brightest colors to find a green which pleases him. The visitors at the Louvre think I'm crazy.

"Amazing! Do you see the painting in that color?" — "Certainly, don't you see that it's all green?"

Portrait of the Painter James Tissot, 1868. Oil on canvas.

Mantegna:
Minerva Driving the Vices
from the Garden of Virtue,
1504. Tempera on canvas.

Finally, the underpainting is finished with much difficulty. The composition is complicated and the placement of all those figures had given me lots of trouble.

During that time, Degas said to me: "But you'll never finish this, I've begun a copy at my studio; I've already nearly finished the drawing; come and see it..."

I go to his studio, and he then shows me a canvas on which he was doing an underdrawing in pastel in monochrome, after a photograph. Right in front of me, passionately fervent, he applied several accents to his underdrawing. He then left it in this state.

This canvas passed through his sale with the attribution "French School." I came across it again shortly after the war at a dealer's; he had paid 200 francs for it. (At the time I was in the army at Châlons and couldn't attend the sale.) The dealer himself had recognized the work of Degas, and naturally charged me a much higher price for it. (Even as it remains, it is a precious souvenir for me.)

When my underdrawing is finished, we take it to the rue de Lisbonne to let it dry in the courtyard. At the end of three months, we take it back to the Louvre, and we plan a rendezvous to apply the glazes.

I arrive on the prearranged day, and all day long I await my Degas, who can't decide to appear. Not knowing what he wanted me to do exactly, I didn't touch my canvas. The next day I return to the Louvre, to wait for him again. Finally there he comes, walking hurriedly, skating on the parquet floors of the Louvre, balancing the large sleeves of his Inverness cape as a bird its wings.

"What? You haven't done anything yet?" — "But I was waiting for you..."

Some grumbling, and, on my part, a rather confused silence. In sum, he would have liked me to go floundering around on my canvas, while he would have come later to give me some masterful directions. But because I hadn't done anything, we had to get started.

We take a fine red which we spread out in a glaze on the green of the underpainting in order to obtain the flesh tones. That didn't work very well. We add raw Sienna, we mess around a little more. Finally he leaves, saying to me, "You will apply all these tones (the blues, reds, yellows) very lightly, as in watercolor, to allow the underlying layers to appear, and that will work very well."

I struggled as best I could on this unhappy canvas, and I must admit that the result was not very brilliant. The excess medium used in its execution made the painting yellow terribly. The copy of a Carpaccio, which I had done previously in a less systematic way, seemed to me to have succeeded better. I must say that the technique of the original Carpaccio was much closer to what Degas had in mind. The Mantegna, painted in egg, is of a completely different technique, and I think that my dear master made a mistake in wanting to have me paint it in the Venetian way or at least in a manner which he thought was like it (Ernest Rouart, quoted by Paul Valéry, *Degas, Danse, Dessin*, 1937).

It certainly seems that if Degas was interested in all the old techniques, Dutch, Florentine, Venetian, it was the last which preoccupied him most particularly towards the end of his life. But, as the preceding anecdote shows, his ideas concerning this technique lacked certainty.

The famous "Venetian technique" has excited the curiosity and envy of many an artist. Nevertheless, even in Venice, there doesn't seem to have been a perfect continuity in the transmission of the techniques of the painting process. Even in the eighteenth century the craft of Tiepolo, for example, is no longer that of Titian, of Veronese, or of Tintoretto. The studio recipes which the Venetians of today have been able to inherit from their predecessors certainly do not constitute the whole of a technique, which would confer on the production of its possessors the so rightly sought after paintwork of the great masters of the sixteenth century.

One can find in old books some indications as to the working methods of the great Venetian masters. But they are unhappily too imprecise and too incomplete.

Anyway, one may gather from the accounts of Boschini that after having carried out the drawing, the Venetians made an underpainting with solid colors which were to serve as the basis for the coloring of the flesh, for the accents of the shadows, and for the highlights which they glazed over the underpainting after waiting until it was well dried.

The same writer tells the story that Tintoretto underpainted his entire canvas in chiaroscuro and that he then colored it piece by piece from nature.

Elsewhere Boschini speaks of the extreme clarity of Veronese's underdrawing, who colored all of it with half-tones, then went over it with free and luminous brushstrokes.

Mrs Merrifield, a more recent author cited above, has attempted to clear up this question.

She was able to gather together some information about Titian from a Milanese restorer. The truth of this information is of course disputable. According to the restorer, Titian applied a chiaroscuro underpainting which he then put aside for five or six months, after which he glazed the flesh tones. Thus he dried out his canvas between each operation of its execution, reglazing and then leaving his canvas to dry until he was satisfied with his work, waiting each time for it to be dry and hard. The underpainting was carried out in cool tones and the warm tones were only glazed onto them.

According to all these historians of painting, including Sir Charles Eastlake, another English author of the nineteenth century and a specialist on these questions, the principle of painting in the Venetian style appears to consist in making an underpainting by painting opaque objects with thick, matt, opaque colors, and in going over this preparation, once it has dried, with half tones and glazes.

The Venetian technique is essentially different from the Flemish underpainting of Rubens, for example, which was a transparent grisaille on which the latter worked most frequently wet into wet.

The great advantage in the Venetian method was to permit the artist to redo his work as often as he wished. In addition, this opaque

Ballet Scene, c. 1885. Oil on canvas.

underpainting allowed as much subtlety in the cool tones as in the warm tones. Actually, the Venetians obtained the latter or the former by spreading out a glaze either more or less dark than the lower layer. It is a well-known principle that the same color, seen transparently, can appear warm or cold depending on whether it is darker or lighter than the underlying layer. The example of smoke, given by Leonardo da Vinci, is typical. Seen against a luminous sky, it appears brown, while passing over black it appears blue.

With their light grisaille, which wasn't opaque, the Flemings could obtain warm colors by this technique, but they must have had recourse to other means for the cool colors.

If later generations of artists knew of these general rules, they were ignorant of the precise way in which the old masters had put them into practice. It is certain that some aspect of the old techniques eluded them, whether in the use of the materials, or in the proportions of the mixtures of varnish with the colors, for example, because they never succeeded in obtaining the paintwork of their models.

Before Degas numerous artists were preoccupied with this research, and among them Reynolds was certainly one of those whom it fascinated the most.

In the account of Reynolds preceding the edition of his complete works, his biographer relates that "he wished so eagerly to know the painting technique of the Venetian painters that he sacrificed excellent pictures of that school, rubbing off the different layers of paint, the better to understand their arrangement."[19] Like them, Reynolds carried out his underpainting with a rich paste application. He did many experiments with different media in order to obtain opaque bases in which the paint would remain firm and the surface clean without undergoing the softening characteristic of layers of oil paint. It was to produce this effect that he mixed in with his paints different varnishes made up of the most varied of resins.

First he used megilp, a mixture of drying oil and of mastic varnish, a medium much in use by the English school. It is probably the use of this medium that produced the firm and precise touch seen in the works of the great English landscape artists. Reynolds also often used copaiva balsam for his underpaintings which exists in its natural state as a viscous paste (like an already prepared varnish), and consequently has no need of being dissolved in an essential oil to be used in painting.

Prudhon, advised by Mérimée, also experimented with varnish mixed with paint. He painted his *Christ on the Cross* (Louvre) with copal varnish. "We shall see in due course what effect it will have produced," says Mérimée.[20] Certainly one can see how badly this technique turned out, which proves that Mérimée was mistaken.

Ingres was not indifferent to these issues. One finds the following passage in his notes: "The Venetian painting technique was revealed to me through a sketch by Mr Lewis, an English painter. That sketch had been made after the beautiful Titian of our museum, *Jesus Carried to the Tomb*. In order to succeed in imitating the master, the artist painted on a canvas with no other imprimatura than a light tone in animal glue, as it appears all artists used it, and, most often, by spreading this color on duck or twill. He recognized that in order to obtain transparency and a good warm tone, it was necessary to glaze everything, in consequence to paint all the lower layer in a gray monochrome like a grisaille: (1) the untouched flesh tones in a very light violet-gray, the brown flesh tones in a stronger gray, and the hair the same way; (2) the green draperies in yellow, the blues in white, the same for the reds and the sky. In general it's necessary to paint harshly, abruptly and straightforwardly. One can do a very light underpainting, always according to this same technique; but at the second layer one must apply it energetically and thickly. The painting thus prepared must express, in spite of its monotony, a feeling of color. One must let it dry at least one full month before returning to it to finish it, and then paint all in glazes, except for white cloths."[21]

In contrast to Reynolds who had studied the question in books and who knew the old and modern treatises, Degas followed his quest solely by studying the works of art whose technique he wished to discover.

Woman Having her Hair Done, c. 1892-1895. Oil on canvas.

He had read nothing on this subject and he let himself be guided only by his instinct as a painter and the science that he had acquired by practice. He operated empirically and tentatively.

It is certain that he made innumerable tests with the materials he used, especially in attempting to determine their correct proportions. But he kept all this cooking secret. He hid it even from those closest to him and never liked it when they tried to stick their noses into it.

All of this puttering about often made him ruin canvases. At other times it helped him achieve powerful coloring. But no more than with Reynolds did it help him rediscover the paintwork of the Venetians.

Shortly before 1900 and still under the influence of his ideas concerning the craft of the old masters, Degas wanted to press his experiments in these directions even farther. He prepared two large canvases with underpaintings, the *Dancer Bowing* and the *Half-Length Dancers*. According to the witnesses who saw them at that time in his studio, the underpaintings were magnificent. Unhappily, since his vision was bothering him considerably, he couldn't complete them as he would have liked, and in retouching the first he made it lose much of its grandeur and brilliance. Meanwhile the four half-length dancers have remained a masterly work despite their incompleteness.

One can cite in addition as canvases of the same period but of smaller dimensions, the *Woman Having Her Hair Done* and the *Milliners*.

In spite of these very interesting experiments, one must recognize that Degas was unable to realize in oil paint what he achieved in pastel.

The first reason is that in pastel he could rapidly and indefinitely fix each layer and continue the work immediately without his eagerness and impetus being cooled by doing it. Whereas with oil, in order to obtain the same result, he had to let each layer dry perfectly before painting over it, which prolonged the procedure and allowed him time to become disgusted with the work. Furthermore, in order to carry out this highly complicated craft of oil painting himself, for which he was getting an intuitive sense by studying the canvases of the old masters but which he didn't know how to achieve in actual practice, he had to necessarily make tentative efforts, even errors, which his seriously affected vision and his age didn't allow him to overcome.

What works wouldn't he have left us in this medium if these obstacles and the demand for "articles" more suitable for sale, as he called them himself, hadn't conspired to paralyze his efforts?

Women Seated on the Terrace of a Café (detail), 1877. Pastel over monotype.

MONOTYPES

Degas devised a curious technique intermediate between painting, pastelwork and printmaking which proved to be a very useful method of expression. Although he hated the term adopted for his procedure, it is difficult not to employ "monotype" since the word has been so long consecrated by use.

According to Degas, the idea for the procedure came to him one day when he was at the printmaker's studio overseeing the printing of his etchings. Watching the printer wipe the plate so that the black ink would remain only in the etched crevices, Degas conceived the notion of inking an unvarnished, unworked copper plate and working in the black coating with a stiff brush. Putting his idea into action, he found that the brush enabled him to partially lift off the ink to produce halftints or entirely remove it to obtain the highlights. In some places he left the black intact to achieve the sort of powerful shadows and deepnesses of night that give his monotypes such an arresting effect.

When the brushwork was completed, the plate was passed through the press as if it were an etching. In principle only one proof should be expected from this process, since logically all of the ink would be transferred to the paper. But Degas examined the plate after this printing and finding a few traces of ink, attempted to pull one and in some cases two more impressions.

These last impressions were naturally very pale. The artist stowed them away in a portfolio, perhaps with the idea of using them one day, as indeed he often did later.

Degas put touches of pastel on the grisaille furnished by the slightly inked paper, sometimes producing simple heightened monotypes and other times doing very worked and finished pieces for which the monotype served only as a point of departure.

The first series of monotypes done by inking the whole plate comprised an entire gamut of possibilities, including impressions that were left entirely in black and white such as *The Fireplace*, *Reclining Woman*, *Woman in a Bathtub*, *The Toilette*, and a frieze of *Dancers*; others which were lightly heightened, such as the *Head of a Singer at the Café-Concert*; and finally true pastels executed on top of a monotype like *The Measured Step*, the *Dancer on the Stage*, or the *Women Seated on the Terrace of a Café*.

The Fireplace, c. 1880. Monotype.

Woman in a Bathtub Sponging her Leg, c. 1883. Pastel over monotype.

Women Seated on the Terrace of a Café, 1877. Pastel over monotype.

The Customer, c. 1879.
Monotype in black ink on paper.

Madam's Birthday Party, 1878-1879.
Monotype in black ink heightened with pastel.

Later on, rather than ink the entire plate and lift the highlights and halftones with a brush or cloth pad, Degas drew his subject in brush with black diluted with spirits. This procedure could not give him the deep blacks admired in the preceding series, but did permit the creation of a drawing that is more precise and more accentuated in its contours.

Degas used this second method for the series of brothel scenes and for the set of thirty-seven monotypes intended to illustrate *Les Petites Cardinal* of Ludovic Halévy.

Among the monotypes executed in this manner are found simple black and white impressions like *Waiting* or *The Customer*, others lightly retouched such as *Madam's Birthday Party*, and some from the *Petites*

Cardinal series which exhibit extensive enhancement such as the one depicting Ludovic Halévy speaking with Madame Cardinal.

Finally, Degas also employed a third procedure. In this case, he did not draw his plate entirely in black but used many tints which were either colored inks or, what is more probable, oil paints. He then worked in pastel on these proofs, almost covering the print. It was in this manner that he executed all the landscapes which he did during a journey in a gig with Bartholomé in 1890, and which were exhibited in 1893 at Durand-Ruel's, rue Laffitte.

Ludovic Halévy
and Madame Cardinal,
c. 1880.
Pastel over monotype.

In his memoir of Degas, Georges Jeanniot tells about the creation of these works.

Degas was delighted with his trip. He had, with his remarkable memory, noted different aspects of nature which he reconstructed from his recollections during the few days that he spent among us. Bartholomé was dumbfounded to see him drawing landscapes as if he still had them before his eyes:

— And note, he said, that Degas did not stop me once to allow him to consider them at his leisure!

— And now, lead me to your studio, Degas said to me, leaving the table.

When he entered, his face took on an expression of pleasure and well-being even though this country studio, installed at the top of our house, could not have been more simple. The doorways and windows had the pitch of the roof. In all, it was an attic with a few old pieces of furniture, two or three easels, a divan with cushions, an etching press (which attracted him immediately), a portable heater, and all that is required for printmaking.

— This is excellent! he cried. We'll work in your studio like Swiss clockmakers. You have paper, ink, the printer's brush with your initials! Bless my soul! Then it's serious? This dabber is magnificent and good in the hand. Let's go! Do you have a smock?

— Yes, and a brand new printer's apron.

— Your press must be difficult with its one crank?

Landscape, 1890.
Monotype and pastel
on paper.

— Yes, but we have muscles!

— Your studio is charming.

I put the apron on him; he had taken off his jacket and rolled up his sleeves.

— Do you have copper or zinc plates?

— Here.

— It's perfect. I must ask you for a piece of cloth to make a dabber suited to my particular purpose; I have wanted to make a series of monotypes for such a long time.[22]

Once supplied with all that he required, without waiting, without allowing himself to be distracted from his idea, he began. With his strong but beautifully shaped fingers, his hand seized the objects, tools of genius, handling them with a unique facility. One saw rising little by little from the metal surface a valley, a sky, white houses, fruit trees with black branches, white birches and oaks, ruts full of water from the recent storm, orange clouds scudding in a turbulent sky above a red and green earth.

All this ordered itself, joined up together, the tones bordered each other in brotherhood and the handle of the brush traced clear forms in the fresh color.

These fine things came into being with no apparent effort, as if he had the model before him.

Bartholomé recognized the places where they had passed at the speed of the white horse's trot.

Landscape with Cows
in the Foreground,
c. 1880-1890.
Pastel on paper.

At the end of a half-hour, scarcely more, Degas's voice proposed:

— We'll go, if you'd like, and pull this proof. Is the paper dampened? Do you have the sponge? You know that the soft-sized paper is best!

— Be calm, I have guaranteed china.

— He has china paper! Let's see this paper.

I deposited a majestic roll on the corner of the table.

When all was ready, the plate placed on the press, the paper applied to the plate, Degas said, "What an agonizing moment! Let it roll! Let it roll!" It was an ancient press with a heavy cross wheel.

The proof obtained, it was suspended on a string where it dried. We did about three or four each morning.

Then he asked for pastel colors to finish the monotypes, and it was then, even more than in the creation of the print, that I admired his taste, his imagination, and the freshness of his memory. He recalled the variety of forms, the construction of the terrain, the unforeseen oppositions and contrasts, it was delicious!

This description by Jeanniot is very interesting because it recounts in a precise way how Degas proceeded in the execution of this series of monotypes.

Although all the monotype methods discussed above are analogous, the third procedure is quite different from the other two. Since the third method requires several colors, each of which must be put in its proper place, Degas could not uniformly ink the entire plate as he did in the first series. Furthermore, it was only after each tint had been properly positioned that the artist could employ the stiff brush used in the first series to create halftones and highlights. Finally, although the third method could be associated with the second since both procedures include a sketch executed with a soft brush, it should be noted that the design of the third series was sketched in a much broader manner than that of the second series.

As one can see, the idea to create a monotype was totally spontaneous and Degas firmly believed that he was the first to use the procedure.

According to Bartsch, however, G.B. Castiglione had already practiced this method:

"Occasionally one finds works by Castiglione that resemble aquatints. However, this type of etching had not yet been invented, so

Landscape, 1890-1892. Pastel.

these prints must have been produced by a different procedure. We believe we have determined the method by which these prints were executed.

"According to our opinion, Castiglione greasily coated a plate of polished copper with oil colors and removed them with a wooden stick in proportion to the halftints and highlights required by his design. After a design had been produced in this manner, he printed the plate in the usual fashion. The prints made in this way naturally were unique, since the black placed on the plate was entirely removed by the paper on the first impression. This theory accounts for the pieces by Castiglione that resemble the prints charged with black that one sometimes finds among those of Rembrandt and of which those by Castiglione are in a way imitations."[23]

In this discussion, Bartsch has incontestably presented the principle of the first series of monotypes executed by Degas. However, as Bartsch says himself, his theory is not a proven certitude but only a hypothesis resulting from the examination of prints. Indeed, it is possible that Castiglione found an unknown way to obtain halftones with acid without his discovery having been officially recognized. In this case, the credit for the invention of monotypes goes to Bartsch.

Be that as it may, it is absolutely certain that Degas was not acquainted with this text.

COUNTERPROOFS

Degas was also fond of counterproofs.

This practice was commonly used by the painters of the eighteenth century for their red chalk drawings but today is generally used only for printmaking.

Degas resurrected it for his drawings in charcoal and his sketches in pastel.

The procedure consists in placing the drawing against an unmarked sheet and then passing the unit through the press. Traces of charcoal or pastel stay on the new sheet, thus giving a reversed and very pale proof.

Degas retouched this proof, and it is very possible that it was sometimes the point of departure for complete pastels.

Counterproofs also could be used to reveal the symmetry of a design, a benefit Degas certainly sought.

Some of these counterproofs passed to the auctioneers of Degas's studio under the designation "Prints in black and color retouched by Edgar Degas."

PRINTMAKING

It is useful to dedicate a few pages to techniques that Degas employed in his prints since these were sometimes quite peculiar to him.

Whatever has been written by Loys Delteil on the subject, it seems that Degas etched his first plates in Rome under the guidance of his friend the engraver Joseph Tourny.[24]

The etchings executed in that period are pure etchings and do not present any peculiarity in their technique. Examples include a *Self-Portrait* in the manner of Rembrandt, the *Portrait of Joseph Tourny*, *Little Nathalie Wolkonska*, the *Sportsman Mounting a Horse*, and *The Roadstead*.

Degas next used another common procedure, etching retouched with drypoint, for the *Infanta Isabella* after Velázquez.

The portrait of his sister, *Madame Fèvre*, is also etched by classic methods. However, it serves as evidence that even at this early date Degas already loved to submit his plates to numerous changes. If in the first state the lines of the face were too pale, it is regrettable that the artist did not believe it worthwhile to keep the second state which was perfect. In the following states he made the print too charged and heavy, destroying this delightful small portrait.

Up to this point Degas had not shown any particular originality in the research of this medium. At best, he was contented to use the common procedure of retouching etchings with drypoint. However, his

Self-Portrait, 1857.
Etching, fourth state.

Portrait of the Engraver Joseph Tourny, 1857.
Etching, one state.

curiosity about the artifice of this craft and his love of tinkering and manual labor quickly gave him the idea of finding new ways to attack copper, a metal rich in resources and interesting to work.

Degas tried the usual method of graining by aquatint, but naturally could not constrain himself to use it in the usual printmaker's fashion which was far too regular for his taste.

His first use of aquatint appears in the *Bust Portrait of Manet*. The first states are worked only with the needle and leave the background and suit clear. In the fourth state these areas are covered by resin grains.

Degas executed the *Portrait of Alphonse Hirsch* in the same way: apparently for the first state the head was worked entirely with the needle and the cravat and suit were added last in aquatint.

For *Behind the Firescreen* and the *Two Dancers*, it seems that Degas did not use resin grains but obtained the overall light tone by momentarily immersing the bare plate directly in acid. The globe seen in the first of these etchings must have been reserved with varnish. A very faint design was executed in drypoint and the other whites were brought out with a burnisher.

As in the *Bust Portrait of Manet*, the tone of the aquatint serves as the background in the *Singer's Profile*, while the face is drawn with a needle.

Bust Portrait of Edouard Manet,
c. 1861.
Etching and aquatint, fourth state.

Behind the Firescreen, 1877-1878.
Aquatint, drypoint and burnisher.

Two Dancers, 1877-1878.
Aquatint, drypoint and burnisher.

The *Dancers in the Wings* presents a more complicated work in aquatint with numerous and successive retouchings using both needle and resin. Eight states of this work are known, during the course of which the number of dancers was varied and the stage was enriched by the curious rocks in the foreground.

The large print *At the Ambassadeurs* presents a complicated melange of different procedures. The use of softground can be detected, followed by accentuation of the design using a needle in some areas and aquatint grains in others. The latter are placed quite irregularly in order to avoid the monotony that is frequently produced by the aquatint process and which can give its proofs the appearance of a photogravure.

Café-Concert at the Ambassadeurs, c. 1876-1877. Pastel over monotype.

This mixture of resin grains with other methods of etching is also found in *The Actresses' Dressing-Room*.

The plate representing *Mary Cassatt at the Louvre* is a typical example of the transformations to which Degas submitted his etched works. One must attentively examine the proofs of the twenty successive states of this plate to distinguish the modifications, the additions and the "erasures" for which Degas used the needle, resin grains and burnisher. For example, one can chart the metamorphoses of the wall panel that

Mary Cassatt at the Louvre (The Gallery of Paintings), 1879-1880.
Etching, softground etching, aquatint and drypoint, first state.

Etching and drypoint, tenth state.

occupies the left portion of the image. At first, it was decorated with marbling produced in aquatint. Then this marbling began to wear down and was reinforced. At this point the panel began to grow, hiding more of the seated figure. It lost its aquatint marbling which was replaced by decorations in drypoint. These last elements were themselves modified, then replaced in their turn by zigzag decorations. The zigzag embellishments were soon covered with a deposit of aquatint grains, light at first, then heavier. Finally the panel was simplified and decorated

Mary Cassatt at the Louvre
(The Etruscan Gallery),
1879-1880.
Softground etching, drypoint,
aquatint and etching, second state.

with vertical scorings executed with the needle. Analogous changes may be observed in the figures, the floor, the ceiling molding and the partition covered with paintings.

The other plate representing Mary Cassatt at the Louvre (in the Etruscan Gallery this time) did not undergo as many changes. However, the first state comprises only two figures of which one is a simple line drawing on an absolutely untouched background, while in the last states almost the entire surface of the plate has been covered. The seated figure was progressively shaded. Then, at the outset of the third state, a tone in aquatint covered the plate. Highlights were obtained by reserving some areas with varnish and by wearing down the grain from the aquatint with a burnisher. Finally, cuts appear on the floor and on the book.

Leaving the Bath (the one in which a woman has one leg in the tub and one on the floor) also exhibits numerous transformations undergone over the course of seventeen states. The aquatint process was used once again, in this case to effect changes in the design of the rugs, the cloth hanging from the chimney, and even in the woman's body (as seen in one of the last states). This plate was initially sketched with one of the rods made of gas carbon used in the electric industry. The first states exhibit this mode of work alone and it was only later that Degas supplemented it with work in aquatint. This first use of the carbon from an arc lamp was completely fortuitous, the result of not having other tools available to attack the copper. One evening a heavy frost had prevented Degas from returning home after a dinner with Alexis Rouart and the artist had to stay overnight with his friend. In the morning, as he expressed the desire to make a print, his host, who lived next door to his factory, found the gas carbon there which enabled Degas to etch the copper he had been given.

Degas was very fond of using carbon from arc lamps for etching and one finds many plates on which it has been used for details and sometimes as the sole procedure.

An example is the small *Portrait of Hélène André* in which she stands with a book in her hand. Here the copper was worked only with a gas carbon rod. The absence of further embellishments gives the print an unstudied appearance, full of charm.

It is the same case for the *Two Dancers in the Wings*. Like *Hélène André*, this print has the appearance of a work from life, a spontaneous record of one's first impressions, even though it is actually a second state. It has nonetheless been executed as lightly as the first print, again using only the gas carbon rod.

The print called *The Small Dressing-Room* was produced with the same tool. Despite the fact that the print exists in four states and has a more worked appearance, the plate was not treated by other methods.

In other plates Degas used this tool as an accessory method to model certain figures or to treat details.

In *Mary Cassatt at the Louvre (The Etruscan Gallery)*, one sees that in the first state Degas used the gas carbon for the entire dress and hat of the standing woman and for a few scattered details on the seated woman.

It seems that Loys Delteil was mistaken when he designated *The Lovers* and *Bust of a Woman* as executed with an arc lamp carbon. These prints rather have the appearance of two states of a plate that was treated with acid, but of which the bite was ineffectual.

Indeed, Degas is said to have purposefully failed the acid treatment of some aquatints. It would be interesting to identify the instances, although it is impossible to be certain in which areas he made use of this technique. It is said that in order to obtain highlights in a plate or part of a plate that had been treated as an aquatint, he flattened the resin with a piece of wood which he had previously warmed. As a result the resin no longer had a granular quality but was a continuous paste, consequently preventing the acid from attacking the metal in areas worked in this fashion.

Degas was very fond of softground, and if he could have given himself more completely to printmaking, he certainly would have made much use of this procedure.

Degas used a traditional softground technique in several plates such as the small portrait of his brother René, the second and third etchings called *On the Stage*, the preliminary design for a program for the soirée of the former students of the Nantes high school, and the *Three Nude Dancers Putting on their Shoes*. He could also use softground in an unusual fashion such as that seen in the large plate of the *Café-Concert* which

The Lovers, c. 1879.
Softground etching.

Bust of a Woman, c. 1879.
Softground etching.

116

A Singer, 1877-1878.
Softground etching and aquatint,
third state.

Delteil calls *At the Ambassadeurs* (discussed above). Besides an occasional grain of aquatint and retouches in etching this print features a unique use of softground: supposedly Degas swept the ground with a brush while it was still fresh. But this is only a hypothesis.

Finally, the print *A Singer* includes a line drawing for the figures and a few areas executed in softground, with the addition for the background of a light grain of aquatint or of aquatint in alcohol. In this last case the resin grains on the plate are slightly dissolved in alcohol which in evaporating leaves a deposit of infinitesimal particles of resin.

Degas did not produce many lithographs but the process was apparently attractive to him. He was often heard to repeat, "If Rembrandt had been acquainted with lithography, God knows what he would have done with it!" This statement certainly implies that Degas held the procedure in great esteem.

But he was asked for paintings, not prints, which explains why his printed oeuvre did not comprise a greater number of pieces. Degas was never able to satisfy his marked penchant for black and white.

On stone as on copper, he could not be content with common procedures, once again conceiving curious methods of expression.

However, due to his remarkable draughtsmanship, even plates executed in simple lithographic crayon following the traditional method produced very beautiful prints. These are *The Dog Song, The Singer of the Café-Concert, Orchestra Loge* and *In the Wings*.

In other works he used a common procedure of placing or spreading lithographic ink with a brush to give body to some of the blacks. This technique is seen in *At the Ambassadeurs*.

However, Degas did invent at least one procedure to be used for lithographs which gave him curious effects and which he would have willingly systematized had he had the chance. The method involved a monotype printed on transfer paper. Using a brush, Degas drew in a suitable ink on a fresh copper plate. The resulting monotype plate would be printed on transfer paper using an etching press. The lithographic printer then transferred this design to a stone which Degas retouched with the scraper, lithographic crayon, and other typical tools.

This type of work furnished the greatest number of his lithographs, giving them a very different look from ordinary ink on stone. It was in this way that Degas treated (among others) plates with two or more subjects, like the *Circus* and the *Woman at the Bedroom Door*, the three renditions of *Mademoiselle Bécat at the Ambassadeurs*, the *Singer of the Café-Concert* and the *Morning Frolic*, the four *Woman's Heads, The Toilette*, the *Portrait of Desboutin*, and *The Café-Concert*. The two plates *After the Bath*, the *Waiting Maid Combing Out Hair*, and the large *Leaving the Bath* were also very probably executed in the same manner.

It is clear that printmaking was attractive to Degas because it was a way of working, retouching and transforming a plate indefinitely while at once conserving the impressions of successive states. He certainly was not interested in obtaining many identical examples of the same state.

DRAWING

Since the purpose of this study is purely technique, it is difficult to expand upon the subject of Degas's drawings. Although there are precious and important observations to make on his method of drawing, remarks concerning even this technique boil down to only a few comments.

In his youth Degas used graphite with a finely shaven point. He made magnificent studies in this medium which can only be compared to those of the great masters. Their pure line could be attributed to Ingres if the sentiment of the form and the inspiration which animated these works didn't differentiate them from the drawings left by the Master of Montauban.

In this series one may group all the drawings done in Italy after the Primitives and the painters of the Renaissance (Mantegna, Botticelli, Benozzo Gozzoli, Lorenzo di Credi, Signorelli, Paolo Uccello, Raphael, Michelangelo, Leonardo da Vinci), the studies of nudes which he did from life while in Italy, the preliminary studies for *Semiramis*, and finally the portraits of Countess Falzacappa and of Madame Gobillard. To this same series one can add the very concise studies of horses which he did a little later.

At this time Degas used the "stone of Italy" (black chalk) as well, notably in his nude studies for the *Misfortunes of the City of Orleans*.

Nude study for The Misfortunes
*of the City of Orleans, 1865.
Black chalk.*

During this period graphite was his preferred drawing medium, as in the *Young Woman Embroidering*. He seems to have abandoned it slowly as his altering vision made the lines drawn by this method seem too pale. Degas then began to use greasy crayons which left stronger blacks on the paper. He increasingly used vine charcoal as well, and at the end of his life it became almost his only method of drawing. He especially favored this medium for the successive tracings which he multiplied for a single composition, a single subject, even a single movement.

The use of tracing paper, which can be considered a working method rather than a technical procedure, seems worthy of discussion here if only to show how Degas used it to execute the masterly pastels which occupied the last productive period of his life.

Young Woman Embroidering, 1855-1860. Pencil heightened with white.

Madame Hertel, 1865. Pencil.

Diego Martelli, 1879. Pencil.

The son of his friend the painter Luigi Chialiva, the architect Jules Chialiva, is said to have given the idea of this practice to Degas. In a letter addressed to the Société de l'Histoire de l'Art Français, Jules Chialiva describes the circumstance in which he involuntarily and indirectly suggested this method to his father's friend:

I brought my first sketch to the house. My father, wanting to correct it, went to retouch the drawing itself, when I stopped him by asking him to make his correction on superimposed tracing paper as practiced at the studio. My father was struck by the advantages of this method of comparison, of the time saved and of the guarantee of not heavying a drawing or certain details and of not losing a sketch which, a moment later, could please. From the next day forward, upon arriving at his studio my father had the model pose at first nude, then asking the man to slightly modify his movements, corrected himself by successive tracings. He then had the model get dressed and correspondingly dressed his drawings, always by superimposed tracings.

Towards five or six in the evening, while my father was drying the ten or twelve drawings on the wall that he had just fixed, Degas entered the studio.

From that day forward, Degas enthusiastically adopted drawing by superimposed tracings to the point of never drawing by any other method.

This is why many drawings exist of which the duplicates only represent insignificant variations.

Apparently, when Degas began to exhaust himself on a design which his already diseased sight made painful to pursue, he traced the already completed work, correcting himself as he drew. The correction was thereby more clear. He repeated the operation until he was satisfied.

However, rather than transfer his corrected drawing onto an ordinary sheet, he began to cover the tracing paper with pastel, then (as discussed above) he fixed this first layer and took up his work anew. It is in this way that he was led to execute so many pastels on tracing paper at the risk of having them glued to paperboard by his framer to "finish" them.

Soon Degas used tracings even for the execution of pastels. Finding himself lost in the middle of the lines and colors which ended by clashing on his retina, and not wanting to uselessly overwork his drawing, he applied another tracing paper to the one he had already worked and began anew, first only outlining the forms, then covering the new sheet with pastel. This drawing sometimes was a magnificent work and sometimes remained a simple sketch, unless his caprice took it up much later to bring it to completion. This working method explains the considerable number of retouched charcoals and unfinished pastels that were found in his studio after his death.

Another result of his working by successive tracing, which is also perhaps an effect of the weakness of his eyesight, is the progressive enlarging of his drawings. It often happened that he drew the

Dancer Adjusting her Slipper, 1874. Pencil and charcoal.

proportions of his figures larger with each new tracing until he would finally draw almost life size a head originally sketched at approximately the size of an orange.

Is it because he traced his design outside its line or is it because of his difficulty in seeing that he enlarged his first tracing in all directions?

A portrait of a mother and her two children that was first drawn on a sheet of Ingres paper in the end became a huge pastel 63 inches high and 55½ wide, a pastel that was furthermore never finished.

In his *Recollections of a Picture Dealer*, Ambroise Vollard tells the story of a drawing commissioned from Degas by Arthur Meyer to illustrate his copy of *La Maison Tellier*:

"As for Degas, he never finished his drawing, and one can say that this was through excess of conscience. Since he forced himself always to

Woman in the Bathtub, c. 1890-1892.

better a work by repetitions on tracing paper which bordered his original outline, the mock-up that he sent to M. Arthur Meyer ended by measuring 39 inches in height. That is to say that the bibliophile had to give up as lost his awaited illustration. But he did not want to settle for this disappointment. To decorate *La Maison Tellier* he bought a monotype by Degas showing two women on a sofa which adapted itself to the tale of Maupassant far better than a drawing of a dancer."

There could be much to say about the drawing of Degas but it would necessitate touching upon the subject of his method, of his conception of drawing and of his objectives, matters which lead to the more abstract concerns of painting. Any such discussion would originate in art's intellectual bases, then, and does not have a place here.

Woman Standing in the Tub, c. 1895-1900. Charcoal.

Dancer Resting, c. 1880-1882. Pastel.

CONCLUSION

Degas's artistic restlessness demands that his work be studied from a technical point of view.

Tormented by the search for a technique suitable to the ideas he wanted to realize, he was never satisfied. This perpetual discontent, already proven by the innumerable experiments which he never ceased pursuing, is especially manifest in his need to continually retouch his work. He was eager for all methods suitable to favoring this bent, whether it was tracing, printmaking or fixing superimposed layers of pastel.

Materials preoccupied him, and he sought the best medium and the best fixative, the best canvas and the best ground, without ever arriving at a definitive solution.

All his life was passed in experimentation in both the aesthetic as well as in the technical aspects of art.

He was not discouraged by the difficulties nor by the problems which he encountered. On the contrary, he loved to confront them, and he perhaps would have created them had they not existed: "Happily I myself have not found my manner, something I would detest!" he exclaimed upon hearing of a painter who rejoiced in having found his. This statement reveals the temperament of an indefatigable explorer as well as Degas's repugnance for the belief that one has arrived at the goal. He could not renounce the hope of new tasks, of new progress.

Degas himself expressed his restlessness time and time again in his correspondence and in his conversation.

In 1890, in a letter to his friend Valernes, where he excuses his severity with his colleague by the fact that he uses the same severity on himself, he declares: "I was or I seemed hard with all the world by a sort of surrender to the brutality that comes to me from my doubt and my bad temper. I felt myself so badly made, so poorly equipped, so soft, while it seemed to me that my calculations concerning art were so correct."

One day at the Salon, overhearing Degas complain that not one of these painters had ever asked himself what ought to be done in painting, an art critic took advantage of the situation to ask him that question. "If I knew," he answered, "I would have done it long ago. I've spent my entire life trying."

Nothing could define his life better than these words.

NOTES

[1] Copy of a Bellini in the Uffizi, Florence, listed as No. 3 in the catalogue of the third Degas sale, Paris, 1919, there wrongly entitled *The Virgin and the Child Jesus*, measuring 16⅛ by 25⅝ inches; and copy of a fresco by Titian in the Scuola del Santo, Padua, listed as No. 2 in the third Degas sale, Paris, 1919, a painting on canvas measuring 31½ by 18½ inches.

[2] *The Rape of the Sabines*, copy after Poussin's picture in the Louvre, an oil on canvas, 58¼ by 80¾ inches, No. 180 in the first sale of the Henri Rouart Collection, Paris, 1912, No. 56 in the catalogue of the 1937 Degas exhibition at the Orangerie, Paris, from the Marin-Bricka Collection; *Christ between the Two Thieves*, copy after Mantegna's picture in the Louvre, oil on canvas, 26⅜ by 36¼ inches, No. 103 in the catalogue of the first Degas sale, Paris, 1918; *Portrait of Anne of Cleves*, copy of Holbein's picture in the Louvre, oil on canvas, 25⅝ by 18⅞ inches, done about 1872, Durand-Ruel Collection; *Two Heads of Men*, copy of a picture in the Louvre (Italian School), oil on canvas, 17 by 24¾ inches.

[3] Anonymous (14th century), *De arte illuminandi*, chapter XV (in tabulis): "Deinde recipe claram ovorum fractam cum pinzello situlare aut canna scissa et adaptata ad illud, sicut pictores faciunt, et, postquam tota clara facta fuerit spuma, pone desuper tantum de aqua communi sive mista cum vino albo optimo, vel modicum de lixivio, aut simpliciter, quod utrumque est bonum, et prohice post modicum spatium de spuma quam superius faciet, et sic que remanebit erit bona. Recipe ergo de ipsa cum pinzello apto ad hoc, et balnea super dictam assisam sapienter et discrete, ita quod dicta assisa habiliter recipiat aurum vel argentum, ut pictores faciunt quando aurum ponunt."

[4] Cennino Cennini, *Il libro dell'arte* of about 1400, chapter CXXXI: "Come si mette il bolio in tavola, e come si tempera."

[5] Cennini, chapter CLVII: "In che modo dei miniare e mettere d'oro in carta."

[6] Theophilus (late 11th - early 12th century), *Libri III de diversis artibus*, chapter XXVII: "How to grind pigments in oil and gum."

[7] *De arte illuminandi*, chapter XVII: "De clara ovorum et quomodo preparatur."

[8] An example of a drawing retouched in oil by Rubens is one by Polidoro da Caravaggio once in the collection of Sir Peter Lely, then in that of Sir Thomas Lawrence.

[9] Having called in Leonardo da Vinci to decorate some rooms in the Vatican, Pope Julius II (it is said) was curious enough one day, when Leonardo was out, to look into the room which served as the painter's studio. There, instead of the sketches and cartoons which the pope expected to find, all he saw were some retorts and chemical utensils, which he assumed the artist used to make his varnishes. Hence his remark, "This man starts where the others end." See J.F.L. Mérimée, *De la peinture à l'huile*, Paris, 1830. According to Mérimée, this equipment must have served to prepare the siccative oils or to rectify the volatile oil of turpentine.

[10] Marco Boschini, *Le ricche minere della pittura veneziana*. Venice, 1672: "Per il piu [Veronese] poneva gli azzurri a guazzo, e per tal cagione alcuni inavveduti, volendo nettar alcuni de suoi quadri, hanno, non volendo, dipennate alcune piegature de panni, che furono delle piu rare che formassero pennelli giamai."

[11] Mary P. Merrifield, *Original Treatises Dating from the XIIth to the XVIIIth Centuries on the Arts of Painting*, London, 1849: "Titian, it is said, frequently laid on the paint with his fingers and in glazing. When large surfaces were to be glazed, the colour was frequently rubbed on with all the fingers or the flat of the hand, so as to fill the interstices left by the brush and to cover the surface thinly and evenly. Another way of applying the colour with the finger, frequently used for the soft shadows of flesh, was to dip the finger into the colour and draw it once along the surface to be painted with an even movement. These touches were called *sfregazzi*, and were distinguished from the process first described, which was called *velatura*."

[12] Marco Boschini, *Le ricche minere della pittura veneziana*: "Ma il condimento degli ultimi ritocchi era andar di quando in quando, unendo con sfregazzi delle dita negli estremi de chiari, avvicinandosi alle mezze tinte, ed unendo una tinta con l'altra; altre volte con un striscio delle dita pure poneva un colpo d'oscuro in qualche angolo, per rinforzarlo, oltre qualche striscio di rosetto, quasi giaccola di sangue, che invigoriva alcun sentimento superficiale, e cosi andava a riducendo a perfezione le sue animate figure. Ed il Palma mi attestava per verità che nei finimenti dipingeva più con le dita, che con pennelli."

[13] Cennino Cennini, *Il libro dell'arte*, chapter LXVII: "Il modo e ordine a lavorare in muro, cioè in fresco e di colorire o incarnare viso giovenile"; and chapter LXXI: "Il modo di colorire un vestimento in fresco."

[14] Giovanni Paolo Lomazzo, *Trattato dell'arte della pittura*, Milan, 1584.

[15] Sir Theodore Turquet de Mayerne, edited by P.E. Berger, Munich, 1901, pp. 254 and 256.

[16] Sir Roger de Piles, *Eléments de peinture pratique*, Paris, 1684-1685.

[17] Eugène Delacroix, *Journal*, edited by André Joubin, Paris, 1932, 1950, 1980: 22 September 1844, 2 March 1847, 10 June and 17 August 1850, 29 August 1851, 1 June 1852, 15 January 1853, 17 October 1854, 8 May and 11 June 1856.

[18] Giovanni Battista Armenini, *De' veri precetti della pittura*, Ravenna, 1587, book II, chapter IX, quoted and translated into French by J.F.L. Mérimée, *De la peinture à l'huile*, Paris, 1830.

[19] Edmond Malone, *The Works of Sir Joshua Reynolds, Knight*, 3 volumes, London, 1798.

[20] J.F.L. Mérimée, *De la peinture à l'huile*, Paris, 1830.

[21] Vicomte Henri Delaborde, *Ingres, sa vie, ses travaux, sa doctrine, d'après les notes manuscrites et les lettres du maître*, Paris, 1870. Quoted by Henri Guerlin, *L'Art enseigné par les maîtres, la technique, peinture*, Paris n.d.

[22] "I have wanted to make a series of monotypes for such a long time." So Jeanniot quotes Degas as saying, probably by an oversight, for "monotype" was a term, I repeat, that Degas detested and never used.

[23] Adam Bartsch, *Le peintre graveur illustré*, 21 volumes, Vienna, 1803-1821. The quotation given here, brought to my attention by P.A. Lemoisne, is from volume XXI. Giovanni Benedetto Castiglione was born at Genoa in 1616 and died at Mantua in 1670.

[24] Delteil states that Degas etched his self-portrait in 1855 and only met Tourny in 1856, and so concludes that it was not Tourny who initiated Degas into etching; he thinks it must have been Bracquemond who did so. But Delteil gives no evidence for these statements, offers no proof that the self-portrait was done in 1855 or that Degas was unacquainted with Tourny before 1856. What is certain is that Degas did not meet Bracquemond until much later; so it cannot have been he who initiated Degas into etching.

BIBLIOGRAPHY

BOOKS, PERIODICALS, ALBUMS OF REPRODUCTIONS

Loys DELTEIL, *Le peintre graveur illustré*, volume IX: *Edgar Degas*, Paris, 1919.

Ambroise VOLLARD, *Degas*, G. Crès et Cie, Paris, 1924, 1938; *Degas, An Intimate Portrait*, New York, 1927.

Edgar DEGAS, *Lettres de Degas*, edited with notes by Marcel GUÉRIN, preface by Daniel HALÉVY, Bernard Grasset, Paris, 1931.

Paul VALÉRY, *Degas, Danse, Dessin*, Ambroise Vollard, Paris, 1937; Gallimard, Paris, 1938; in English, New York, 1948, 1960.

Ambroise VOLLARD, *Souvenirs d'un marchand de tableaux*, Albin Michel, Paris, 1938; *Recollections of a Picture Dealer*, Boston, 1936.

Jules CHIALIVA, "Comment Degas a changé sa technique du dessin," in *Bulletin de la Société de l'Histoire de l'art français*, 1932.

Georges JEANNIOT, "Souvenirs sur Degas," in *La Revue Universelle*, 15 October and 1 November 1933.

Ernest ROUART, "Degas," in *Le Point*, February 1937.

Vingt dessins de Degas, Boussod, Manzi, Joyant et Cie, Paris, 1896.

Henri RIVIÈRE, *Les dessins de Degas*, Demotte, Paris, 1922-1923.

OTHER WORKS CONSULTED

Giovanni Paolo LOMAZZO, *Trattato dell'arte della pittura*, Milan, 1584, reprinted Rome 1844, 1947.

THEOPHILUS PRESBYTER, *Essais sur divers arts*, edited by Comte Charles de l'ESCALOPIER with a French translation, Firmin-Didot, Paris, 1843, reprinted Paris, 1980; *Libri III de diversis artibus; seu, Diversarum artium schedula*, Latin text with English translation by Robert Hendrie, London, 1847.

De arte illuminandi, edited in Latin by A. LECOY DE LA MARCHE, Ernest Leroux, Paris, 1890; translated into French by Louis DIMIER, Louis Rouart et fils, Paris, 1927; into English, New Haven, 1933.

Cennino CENNINI, *Il libro dell'arte*, early 1400s, Italian edition by Gaetano MILANESI, Florence, 1859; French translation by Victor MOTTEZ, Vve Renouard, Paris, 1885, reprinted 1978; English edition, *The Craftsman's Handbook*, by Daniel V. THOMPSON, Jr., New Haven and London, 1933, reprinted New York, 1954, 1961.

Giovanni Battista ARMENINI, *De' veri precetti della pittura*, Ravenna, 1587.

Marco BOSCHINI, *Le ricche minere della pittura veneziana*, Venice, 1664, enlarged edition Venice, 1672, reprinted Rome, 1844.

Theodore Turquet de MAYERNE, manuscript edited with German translation, Munich, 1901.

Roger de PILES, *Eléments de peinture pratique*, Paris, 1684-1685, edited by Charles-Antoine JOMBERT, Paris, 1766.

Edmond MALONE, *The Works of Sir Joshua Reynolds, Knight*, 3 volumes, London, 1798; French translation by JANSEN, Paris, 1806.

J.F.L. MÉRIMÉE, *De la peinture à l'huile ou Des procédés matériels employés dans ce genre de peinture depuis Hubert et Jan van Eyck jusqu'à nos jours*, Mme Huzard, Paris, 1830; *The Art of Painting in Oil*, London, 1839.

Mary P. MERRIFIELD, *Original Treatises Dating from the XIIth to the XVIIIth Centuries on the Arts of Painting*, 2 volumes, John Murray, London, 1849, reprinted New York and London, 1967.

Sir Charles EASTLAKE, *Materials for a History of Oil Painting*, 2 volumes, London, 1847-1869, reprinted as *Methods and Materials of Painting of the Great Schools and Masters*, 2 volumes, New York and London, 1960.

Vicomte Henri DELABORDE, *Ingres, sa vie, ses travaux, sa doctrine*, Paris, 1870.

Eugène DELACROIX, *Journal*, Plon, Paris, 1893; edited by André JOUBIN, Paris, 1932, 1950, 1980.

Antonin PROUST, *Edouard Manet, Souvenirs*, edited by A. BARTHÉLÉMY, H. Laurens, Paris, 1913.

G. LAFENESTRE, *La vie et l'œuvre de Titien*, Hachette, Paris, 1909.

Emile BERNARD, *Souvenirs sur Paul Cézanne et lettres inédites*, La Rénovation Esthétique, Paris, 1921.

Ambroise VOLLARD, *Renoir*, G. Crès et Cie, Paris, 1920; *Renoir, An Intimate Record*, New York, 1925.

Albert ANDRÉ, *Renoir*, edited by Georges BESSON, G. Crès et Cie, Paris, 1919, 1928.

Henri GUERLIN, *L'art enseigné par les maîtres, la technique, peinture*, Laurens, Paris.

Catalogue des peintures et pastels, Musée du Louvre, Paris.

Catalogue, Musée de Reims.

PUBLISHER'S NOTE: The standard Degas catalogue, P.A. Lemoisne, *Degas et son œuvre*, 4 volumes, Arts et Métiers Graphiques, Paris, 1946-1948, was not yet available when Denis Rouart was writing *Degas à la recherche de sa technique*, first published Paris, 1945.

BIOGRAPHY AND BACKGROUND

1834 Birth of Edgar Degas in Paris, July 19. His father was a banker; his mother, née Musson, came from a French Creole family of New Orleans.

1839 Birth of Cézanne.
1840 Birth of Monet.
1841 Birth of Renoir.

1845 Enrolls at the Lycée Louis-le-Grand, Paris, where he spends all his school years. Beginning of a lifelong friendship with Henri Rouart, his schoolmate.

1847 Death of his mother. Degas's father, a cultured man with a taste for music and painting, takes the boy to the museums and fosters his gift for drawing.

1848 Birth of Gauguin.

1852 Degas converts one room of his father's apartment into a studio.

1853 Having passed his "baccalaureate" and had a brief fling at studying law, he enrolls in Barrias' studio. Copies many pictures in the Cabinet des Estampes and the Louvre.

1853 Birth of Van Gogh.

1854 Degas becomes a pupil of Louis Lamothe, who had studied under Ingres and Flandrin. First visit to Naples, where he stays with his grandfather.

1855 Enrolls at the Ecole des Beaux-Arts, Paris, where he meets Tourny, Bonnat, Elie Delaunay, Fantin-Latour, Ricard.

1856 Travels to Italy, staying in Rome, Naples and Florence until the following year. Pictures of old Italian street-women.

1856 Courbet paints *Young Ladies on the Banks of the Seine*.

1858 Another visit to Rome. In July he sets out on a leisurely trip to Florence, by way of Viterbo, Orvieto (where he copies Signorelli, whose "love of stir and bustle" he admires), Perugia, Assisi. At Florence he stays with his uncle, Baron Bellelli. First studies for the portrait of his uncle's family.

1859 Birth of Seurat.

1860 Under the influence of Ingres and the Italian masters, Degas is strongly drawn to historical painting and soon produces several pictures on legendary and mythological themes.

1860 Large-scale exhibition in Paris of Modern Painting (Delacroix, Corot, Courbet, Millet).

1861 "Semiramis founding a City."

1861 Ingres, now 81, paints the *Turkish Bath*.

1862 Degas strikes up a friendship with Manet. First pictures of jockeys.

> 1863 Salon des Refusés. Manet's *Déjeuner sur l'Herbe*.
> Death of Delacroix.
> 1864 Birth of Toulouse-Lautrec.

1865 "The Misfortunes of the City of Orléans," after which Degas repudiates historical painting. "Woman with Chysanthemums" and many portraits date from this period. Through Manet he meets the young Impressionists-to-be. Gatherings at the Café Guerbois, near the Place Clichy, in which Zola and Duranty also take part.

> 1865 Manet exhibits *Olympia* at the Salon.
> 1867 The Goncourt brothers publish *Manette Salomon*. Birth of Bonnard. Death of Ingres and Baudelaire. Monet's *Women in the Garden*. Courbet exhibition.

1868 "Mademoiselle Fiocre in the Ballet 'La Source'" and "The Orchestra at the Paris Opera."

> 1868 Birth of Vuillard. Corot paints *Woman with a Pearl*.
> 1869 Birth of Matisse. Manet paints *The Balcony*. Renoir and Monet work at Bougival. The impressionist technique takes form.

1870 Called up for duty in the Franco-Prussian War, Degas serves in an artillery unit manning a fortress near Paris.

> 1870 Fantin-Latour paints *The Studio at Batignolles*.

1872 Degas takes to visiting the rehearsal rooms of the opera dancers in the Rue Le Pelletier. In October he sails for New Orleans with his brother René, remaining in the United States until April 1873. "The Cotton Office." "Woman with a Vase of Flowers."

1874 Degas takes an active part in organizing the First Impressionist Exhibition, and shows ten pictures, including "The Dancing Class." Edmond de Goncourt visits his studio and admires his work.

> 1875 Death of Corot.
> 1876 Second Impressionist Exhibition.
> 1877 Third Impressionist Exhibition.
> 1878 Duret publishes *Les Peintres impressionnistes*.
> 1879 Fourth Impressionist Exhibition. Death of Daumier.

1880 Trip to Spain. Etchings with Mary Cassatt and Pissarro.

> 1880 Fifth Impressionist Exhibition. Death of Flaubert.

1881 At the Sixth Impressionist Exhibition Degas shows his first piece of sculpture, a wax statuette of a fourteen-year-old dancing girl. Produces a great many statues in the following years. Does many monotypes and lithographs. More and more pastels.

> 1881 Birth of Picasso.

1882 Several pictures of laundresses and milliners.

> 1882 Seventh Impressionist Exhibition.
> 1883 Death of Manet.

1885 Holiday trip in August to Le Havre and Dieppe, where he and Gauguin have a heart-to-heart talk. His eyesight is giving him serious cause for worry. Concentrates now on painting dancers and nudes, intent on expressing form and rhythmic movement to the exclusion of all else. Breaks new technical ground as he experiments with pastel, tempera, oils mixed with turpentine, using them in all conceivable combinations.

1886 A visit to Naples in January. Eighth and last Impressionist Exhibition in Paris, at which Degas shows a set of nudes of women bathing and grooming themselves.

    1886 Revelation of the Douanier Rousseau at the Salon des Indépendants.
    1887 Lautrec paints his first pictures of Montmartre life.
    1888 Van Gogh at Arles. James Ensor paints the *Entrance of Christ into Brussels*.

1889 Degas travels in Spain with Boldini, then goes on to Morocco.

    1890 Death of Van Gogh.
    1891 First Exhibition of the Nabis. Lautrec's first poster for the Moulin Rouge. Gauguin sails for Tahiti.

1893 Degas shows a series of pastel landscapes, painted from memory after a holiday in the country with Bartholomé the year before. His eyes steadily failing him, he works on only with the greatest difficulty.

    1893 Opening of the Vollard Gallery in Paris.
    1895 First public motion-picture shows given by the Lumière Brothers.

1897 Trip to Montauban to see the works in the Musée Ingres.

1898 Stays with a friend at Saint-Valéry-sur-Somme. Little is known of Degas's last years. He lived in seclusion, seeing only a few friends of long standing: the sculptor Bartholomé, Daniel Halévy, Henri Rouart. He built up a remarkable collection of pictures, in which Ingres and Delacroix enjoyed pride of place. One of the very first to recognize Gauguin's genius, Degas was one of the few to buy Gauguin's work at the Hôtel Drouot auction-sales in 1891 and 1895. Practically blind at the last, he devoted himself to sculpture.

    1899 Group exhibition of the Nabis at Durand-Ruel's in homage to Odilon Redon. Signac publishes *D'Eugène Delacroix au Néo-Impressionnisme*. Death of Sisley.
    1900 Picasso's first stay in Paris.
    1901 Death of Toulouse-Lautrec.

1912 Death of his old friend Henri Rouart. The house in the Rue Victor-Massé, in which Degas had made his home and studio for twenty years and to which he was much attached, is pulled down. His canvases are now fetching very high prices.

1917 Death of Degas in Paris on September 27, at the age of 83.

LIST OF ILLUSTRATIONS

Unless otherwise specified, all the illustrations were made from archive photographs

OTHER ARTISTS

MANET Edouard (1832-1883):

MANTEGNA Andrea (1431-1506):

TEXT AND COLOR PLATES PRINTED BY
IRL IMPRIMERIES RÉUNIES LAUSANNE S.A.

BINDING BY
MAYER & SOUTTER S.A. RENENS

PRINTED IN SWITZERLAND